I0798713

ליבי במזרח
LIBI B'MIZRACH

VOLUME III

המוסיקה של התפילה הישראלית הליברלית
MUSIC OF PROGRESSIVE ISRAELI T'FILAH

Edited by JOEL EGLASH

Executive Committee
CANTOR DAVID BERGER
CANTOR GALIT DADOUN COHEN
JOEL EGLASH
CANTOR CLAIRE FRANCO
CANTOR ROSS WOLMAN

TMP
TRANSCONTINENTAL
MUSIC PUBLICATIONS
A Division of the American Conference of Cantors

לִבִּי בְמִזְרָח וְאָנֹכִי בְּסוֹף מַעֲרָב.

My heart is in the East, yet I am far in the West.

– Y'hudah HaLevi (12th century)

HEBREW PRONUNCIATION GUIDE

VOWELS	CONSONANTS
a as in father	ch as in Bach or Scottish loch (not as in cheese)
ai as in aisle (= long i as in island)	g = hard g as in get (not soft g as in gem)
e as in bed	tz as in boats
ei as in eight (= long a as in ace)	h after a vowel is silent
i as in pizza (= long e as in be)	r = like the Italian (rolled) or French r
o as in go	
u as in lunar	
' = unstressed vowel close to ə or unstressed short e	

LIBI B'MIZRACH: MUSIC OF PROGRESSIVE ISRAELI T'FILAH VOLUME III

Proofread by Cantor David Berger, Cantor Galit Dadoun Cohen, Cantor Claire Franco, and Cantor Ross Wolman
Copyedited by Debra Corman – Music engraved by Josh Wiczer – Design and compositing by Joel Eglash
Cover photograph from Jerusalem's Old City, R'chov HaY'hudim (Jewish Quarter Street)

Transcontinental Music Publications Executive Committee:
—Joel Eglash, Cantor Lauren Phillips Fogelman, Cantor Claire Franco, and Cantor Steven Weiss
American Conference of Cantors: President, Cantor Seth Warner; COO, Rachel Roth
TMP/JLicense Customer Support: Stacey Berliner – TMP/JLicense Production Assistant: Eden Franco

TRANSCONTINENTAL MUSIC PUBLICATIONS
A DIVISION OF THE AMERICAN CONFERENCE OF CANTORS
The world's leading publisher of Jewish music since 1938
1375 Remington Road, Suite M – Schaumburg, IL 60173
847.781.7800 – tmp@accantors.org

Printed in the United States of America – 10 9 8 7 6 5 4 3 2 1
Item number 994070 – ISBN 979-8-9889024-4-7
Includes unique audio download code insert

TranscontinentalMusic.com

Funding for *Libi B'Mizrach Volume III*
was generously provided by

Hebrew Union College–Jewish Institute of Religion
Debbie Friedman School of Sacred Music
Class of 2007

Cantor Devorah Avery
Cantor David Berger
Cantor Mia Fram Davidson
Cantor Shayna De Lowe
Cantor Todd Kipnis
Cantor Elizabeth Sacks
Cantor Randall Schloss
Cantor Billy Tiep
Cantor Ross Wolman
Cantor Anna Zhar

TABLE OF CONTENTS

תוכן העניינים

INTRODUCTION

הַרְחִיבִי מְקוֹם אָהֳלֵךְ וִירִיעוֹת מִשְׁכְּנוֹתַיִךְ. יַטּוּ אַל־תַּחְשֹׂכִי.
הַאֲרִיכִי מֵיתָרַיִךְ וִיתֵדֹתַיִךְ חַזֵּקִי. (ישעיהו נ״ד:ב)

Expand the site of your tent, extend the size of your dwelling.
Do not stint! Lengthen the ropes and drive the pegs firm. (Isaiah 54:2)

To separate the Israeli community in North American denominational terms is simply impossible. The lines dividing between "Progressive," "Secular," "Religious," "Traditional," "Orthodox," and the like just don't work the same way that they do on this side of the ocean. Jewish cultural inspiration flows freely across communities of different religious practice, ethnic identity, and socioeconomic class, realizing one of the great dreams of Zionism—a center of Jewish expression where the treasures of the varied Jewish past and the newest creations of the diverse present mix together in a chaotic harmony. Divisions between groups do, of course, exist, but the universal access to Hebrew as a language of prayer, of poetry, of protest, and of emotional expression opens up infinite possibilities for adoption, adaptation, and assimilation of music across all borders.

It is in this spirit that the executive committee for *Libi B'Mizrach Volume III* has enlarged the size of our tent: expanding beyond the strict limits of music created within Israeli progressive Jewish communities to music representing a broader spectrum of the Israeli Jewish experience. This expansion better reflects the actual musical world of contemporary Israeli synagogues—where traditional *piyut* melodies from Morocco intertwine with new-age chants, and popular songs from the radio combine with Chasidic *nigunim*.

Rabbi David Kimchi (1160–1235, known as the Radak) explained that the tent of our communities described by Isaiah would need to be enlarged because of "all of the children who will come to us." Sometimes, especially in times of conflict, we are inclined to tightly close the sides of our tents to protect ourselves from whatever we feel is "outside." Isaiah, and Kimchi, prophetically remind us that when we open up space, lengthen the ropes, and reinforce the tent pegs that provide strength and stability, the newly created room is filled not by strangers, but by our own children. With this collection, significantly larger than either volumes I or II, we hope to show that the wider perspective shown in these selections is at least one way to bring more of our people, our children, home.

Our hearts are in the East as we look toward Jerusalem, and we stand in the West as communities of Jews working to fill our own tents with an expansive and expanding vision of Jewish life and music. May this volume inspire new sounds and new artistic expressions that fill sanctuaries to the brim, demanding that we honor Isaiah's call to grow wider, deeper, and more inclusive than ever.

Libi B'Mizrach Volume III executive committee
Cantor David Berger, Cantor Galit Dadoun Cohen, Joel Eglash, Cantor Claire Franco, and Cantor Ross Wolman
Passover 2024 / Pesach 5784

דברי מבוא

אִם־אֶשְׁכָּחֵךְ יְרוּשָׁלָֽיִם תִּשְׁכַּח יְמִינִֽי. תִּדְבַּק־לְשׁוֹנִי לְחִכִּי אִם־לֹא אֶזְכְּרֵכִי
אִם־לֹא אַֽעֲלֶה אֶת־יְרוּשָׁלַֽיִם עַל רֹאשׁ שִׂמְחָתִֽי. (תהילים קל״ז:ה׳-ו׳)

If I forget you, O Jerusalem, let my right hand wither, let my tongue stick to my palate if I cease to think of you, if I do not keep Jerusalem in memory even at my happiest hour. (Psalm 137:5-6)

With deep passion and commitment to our musical family in Israel, we present to you this remarkable collection of Israeli songs. The scope of the series has been expanded—building on the success of the first volumes and the experience of creating this volume at a challenging time in Israel's history—to include not only exciting new songs for *t'filah* from diverse Israeli communities and artists from varied religious or secular backgrounds, but from also major commercial songwriters and folk traditions that have seen recent renewed interest.

The pool of *Libi B'Mizrach* songwriters, community leaders, and artists has also grown considerably, and personally speaking, developing these relationships has been the most satisfying endeavor of my career. For the five of us on the volume III executive committee, Israeli music, people, and culture are central parts of our lives. We believe that these masterful creators of music deserve to have their brilliant art and fascinating stories shared with the world.

Publishing Hebrew songs is a crucial part of our mission. To each of us in the Diaspora for whom Hebrew is a supplementary language, these original Israeli melodies and pan-Sephardic *piyutim* (liturgical poems) come straight from the source, with nothing lost in translation. To Western ears, Jewish liturgy, prayers, blessings, and *piyutim* are most purely expressed through the tongue of a native Hebrew speaker.

Until *Libi B'Mizrach*, many of these songs were inaccessible to Westerners or simply unavailable outside of Israel. Now, these beautiful, engaging melodies are presented here in a concise, practical format with highly detailed accuracy. A full accompanying audio album featuring the original artists' recordings is included, and in the back of the book you will find biographical information on the songwriters. This is all meant to help you share their music and stories with your community.

I'd like to make note of the extraordinary accompanying recording to this volume. In addition to securing rights to many of the original artists' recordings, we worked alongside artists to create new productions in Israel. Of particular note are gorgeous new recordings—exclusive to this volume—of six traditional Moroccan and Sephardic songs by the ensemble Be'ayin Mizrachit (more info in the *Songwriters and Communities* index) and new productions from Nava Tehila, Savion Ben Israel, Mordechai Corcos, Maya Raviv, and Amichai Shiryon (performing his and his father's songs). In addition, we produced four new recordings at Congregation Beit Simchat Torah in New York (thank you, CBST!) which were beautifully sung by Cantor Iris Karlin and Cantor Galit Dadoun Cohen.

An incredible crew of contributors worked very hard to make this volume essential. Thank you, truly from my heart, to my partners: the remarkable, brilliant, and dedicated volume III executive committee of Cantor David Berger, Cantor Galit Dadoun Cohen, Cantor Claire Franco, and Cantor Ross Wolman. Cantor Evan Cohen, Cantor Sarah Grabiner, and Cantor Eli Schleifer, our Israeli colleagues, each were invaluable with proofreading, text sources, and on-the-ground assistance. We are all grateful to Josh Wiczer and to the staff and leadership of the American Conference of Cantors and Transcontinental Music Publications, including president Cantor Seth Warner, COO Rachel Roth, and Stacey Berliner.

Sing to us one of the songs of Zion. שִׁירוּ לָנוּ מִשִּׁיר צִיּוֹן.

Joel Eglash
Passover 2024 / Pesach 5784

ליבי במזרח

LIBI B'MIZRACH

VOLUME III

אדון הסליחות

ADON HAS'LICHOT

MUSIC: TRADITIONAL SEPHARDIC (Y'RUSHALMI)
AS SUNG AT KEHILLAT YOZMA (MODI'IN) ED. BE'AYIN MIZRACHIT
TEXT: UNKNOWN

CODA

1. God of forgiveness—You examine the heart,
reveal its depth, speak what is right.

1. אֲדוֹן הַסְּלִיחוֹת, בּוֹחֵן לְבָבוֹת,
גּוֹלֶה עֲמוּקוֹת, דּוֹבֵר צְדָקוֹת.

We have strayed and we have sinned. Show us compassion.

חָטָאנוּ לְפָנֶיךָ רַחֵם עָלֵינוּ.

2. Majestic in wonders, ancient Source of comfort—
You recall our ancestors' covenant, seek out our innermost being.

2. הָדוּר בְּנִפְלָאוֹת, וָתִיק בְּנֶחָמוֹת,
זוֹכֵר בְּרִית אָבוֹת, חוֹקֵר כְּלָיוֹת.

3. Soul of goodness—You bestow goodness and know all mysteries.
Arrayed in righteousness, You overcome sin.

3. טוֹב וּמֵטִיב לַבְּרִיּוֹת, יוֹדֵעַ כָּל נִסְתָּרוֹת,
כּוֹבֵשׁ עֲוֹנוֹת, לוֹבֵשׁ צְדָקוֹת.

4. Perfect with good attributes, awesome in praises.
Forgiver of iniquities, answering those in distress.

4. מָלֵא זַכִּיּוֹת, נוֹרָא תְהִלּוֹת,
סוֹלֵחַ עֲוֹנוֹת, עוֹנֶה בְּעֵת צָרוֹת.

5. Worker of salvation, seer of the future.
Caller of generations, rider upon the heavens.
Answerer of prayers, perfect in knowledge.

5. פּוֹעֵל יְשׁוּעוֹת, צוֹפֶה עֲתִידוֹת,
קוֹרֵא הַדּוֹרוֹת, רוֹכֵב עֲרָבוֹת.
שׁוֹמֵעַ תְּפִלּוֹת, תְּמִים דֵּעוֹת.

אדון עולם

ADON OLAM

MUSIC: BARUCH SHIRYON
AS SUNG AT KEHILLAT YOZMA (MODI'IN)
TEXT: ATTRIBUTED TO SOLOMON IBN GABIROL (11TH C.)

1. אֲדוֹן עוֹלָם אֲשֶׁר מָלַךְ,
בְּטֶרֶם כָּל יְצִיר נִבְרָא.
לְעֵת נַעֲשָׂה בְחֶפְצוֹ כֹּל,
אֲזַי מֶלֶךְ שְׁמוֹ נִקְרָא.

1. You are our Eternal God,
who reigned before any being had been created;
when all was done according to Your will,
then You were called Ruler.

2. וְאַחֲרֵי כִּכְלוֹת הַכֹּל,
לְבַדּוֹ יִמְלוֹךְ נוֹרָא.
וְהוּא הָיָה, וְהוּא הֹוֶה,
וְהוּא יִהְיֶה, בְּתִפְאָרָה.

2. And after all ceases to be,
You alone will rule in majesty.
You have been, are yet,
and will be in glory.

3. וְהוּא אֶחָד וְאֵין שֵׁנִי,
לְהַמְשִׁיל לוֹ לְהַחְבִּירָה.
בְּלִי רֵאשִׁית בְּלִי תַכְלִית,
וְלוֹ הָעֹז וְהַמִּשְׂרָה.

3. And You are One;
none other can compare to or consort with You.
You are without beginning, without end.
To You belong power and dominion.

4. וְהוּא אֵלִי וְחַי גֹּאֲלִי,
וְצוּר חֶבְלִי בְּעֵת צָרָה.
וְהוּא נִסִּי וּמָנוֹס לִי,
מְנָת כּוֹסִי בְּיוֹם אֶקְרָא.

4. And You are my God, my living Redeemer,
my Rock in times of trouble and distress.
You are my standard bearer and my refuge,
my benefactor when I call on You.

5. בְּיָדוֹ אַפְקִיד רוּחִי,
בְּעֵת אִישַׁן וְאָעִירָה.
וְעִם רוּחִי גְּוִיָּתִי,
יְיָ לִי וְלֹא אִירָא.

5. Into Your hands I entrust my spirit,
when I sleep and when I wake,
and with my spirit my body also;
Adonai is with me and I shall not fear.

אדון עולם

ADON OLAM

MUSIC: FROM THE ALGERIAN SONG "YA RAYEH" BY RASHID TAHA
AS SUNG AT KEHILLAT YOZMA (MODI'IN) ED. BE'AYIN MIZRACHIT
TEXT: ATTRIBUTED TO SOLOMON IBN GABIROL (11TH C.)

1. You are our Eternal God,
who reigned before any being had been created;
when all was done according to Your will,
then You were called Ruler.

1. אֲדוֹן עוֹלָם אֲשֶׁר מָלַךְ,
בְּטֶרֶם כָּל יְצִיר נִבְרָא.
לְעֵת נַעֲשָׂה בְחֶפְצוֹ כֹּל,
אֲזַי מֶלֶךְ שְׁמוֹ נִקְרָא.

2. And after all ceases to be,
You alone will rule in majesty.
You have been, are yet,
and will be in glory.

2. וְאַחֲרֵי כִּכְלוֹת הַכֹּל,
לְבַדּוֹ יִמְלוֹךְ נוֹרָא.
וְהוּא הָיָה, וְהוּא הֹוֶה,
וְהוּא יִהְיֶה, בְּתִפְאָרָה.

3. And You are One;
none other can compare to or consort with You.
You are without beginning, without end.
To You belong power and dominion.

3. וְהוּא אֶחָד וְאֵין שֵׁנִי,
לְהַמְשִׁיל לוֹ לְהַחְבִּירָה.
בְּלִי רֵאשִׁית בְּלִי תַכְלִית,
וְלוֹ הָעֹז וְהַמִּשְׂרָה.

4. And You are my God, my living Redeemer,
my Rock in times of trouble and distress.
You are my standard bearer and my refuge,
my benefactor when I call on You.

4. וְהוּא אֵלִי וְחַי גֹּאֲלִי,
וְצוּר חֶבְלִי בְּעֵת צָרָה.
וְהוּא נִסִּי וּמָנוֹס לִי,
מְנָת כּוֹסִי בְּיוֹם אֶקְרָא.

5. Into Your hands I entrust my spirit,
when I sleep and when I wake,
and with my spirit my body also;
Adonai is with me and I shall not fear.

5. בְּיָדוֹ אַפְקִיד רוּחִי,
בְּעֵת אִישַׁן וְאָעִירָה.
וְעִם רוּחִי גְּוִיָּתִי,
יְיָ לִי וְלֹא אִירָא.

אהובי

AHUVI

MUSIC: YONATAN BAR GIORA
AS SUNG BY MIRI MESIKA
TEXT: AHARON PEREZ OF DJERBA (18TH C.)

With deep passion ♩ = 100

38
Am Cm
Em Gm
A-yeih chez-yo - nim. Na-mu ne - e - ma - nim, a - hu-
43
Am7 Cm7
F#m7(b5) Am7(b5)
B7(b9) D7(b9)
B7 D7
VERSES 4&5
Gm Bbm
vi, sho - meir e - mu - nim. 4. Nil - ei - ti n' - so
(5. Par) - tzu ga - deir u -
48
Cm Ebm
ol mo - nim, sav - a - ti ra - bat biz - yo - nim. A - hu - vi, nag-ah che - rev ad g' - ro-
vin - ya - nim, har - su v' - nat - u na - a-ma - nim. A - hu - vi, ak - ru v' - shat-lu kim-sho-
53
Gm Bbm
Cm Ebm
Gm Bbm
nim, Ma-a-rav Do-da-nim, Mo-a-vim, A-mo-nim,
nim. Eich! Tzur g' - o - nim, b'nei a - do - nim,
58
Cm7 Ebm7
D7(b9) F7(b9) Last time to Coda
D7 F7
CHORUS
Gm Bbm
a-hu - vi, E - dom vi - Va - nim. A-hu - vi, E -
a-hu - vi, a - va - dim v'ein ko - nim.
64
Cm6 Ebm6
Cm/Eb Ebm/Gb
3fr
Gm Bbm
Cm6 Ebm6
D7(sus4) F7(sus4)
dom, a-hu - vi, ka - nim, a-hu - vi, sho - meir e-mu - nim,
70
D7 F7
Gm Bbm
Cm6 Ebm6
Cm/Eb Ebm/Gb
D7(sus4) F7(sus4)
D7 F7
D.S. al Coda
a-hu - vi, nag - ah, che-rev ad g'ro - nim. 5. Par -

Beloved, sweet one, brilliant light in the deepest darkness,
the blossom season has arrived.
My beloved, arise to wander through the gardens,
to gather roses, myrrh, and cinnamon,
my beloved, thickets and reeds.

אָהוּב נֶחְמָד, זִיו אִישׁוֹנִים,
הִגִּיעָה עֵת הַנִּצָּנִים.
אֲהוּבִי, קוּמָה לְךָ לִרְעוֹת בַּגַּנִּים,
לִלְקֹט שׁוֹשַׁנִּים, מוֹר עִם קִנְּמוֹנִים,
אֲהוּבִי, קִדָּה וְקָנִים.

Look out and see the view from the heights,
for the waters have swelled ominously.
My beloved, if sins have gone over your head,
remember the boys reared in luscious scarlet.
My beloved, they have wandered from their nests.

הַשְׁקֵף וְהַבֵּט מִמְּעוֹנִים,
כִּי גָבְרוּ מַיִם זְדוֹנִים.
אֲהוּבִי, אִם לְרֹאשׁ עָבְרוּ עֲווֹנִים,
זָכְרָה לְבָנִים עַל תּוֹלָע אֱמוּנִים.
אֲהוּבִי, נָדְדוּ מִקִּנִּים.

My beloved, Edom,
my beloved, reeds,
my beloved, guardian of the faith,
my beloved, a sword is held to the throat.

אֲהוּבִי, אֱדוֹם,
אֲהוּבִי, קָנִים,
אֲהוּבִי, שׁוֹמֵר-אֱמוּנִים,
אֲהוּבִי, נָגְעָה חֶרֶב עַד גְּרוֹנִים.

Enemies and tormentors have raised their hand,
it's been so many days, even years.
My beloved, it has been almost an eternity.
Where are the visions? The faithful are slumbering,
my beloved, guardian of the faith.

I am burdened with a heavy load,
filled by an abundance of humiliations.
My beloved, a sword is held to the throat,
by Arabians, Moabites, Ammonites,
my beloved, Edom and Greece.

They have breached fences and buildings,
destroyed and sowed guilty pleasures.
My beloved, they uprooted and planted thorns.
How so! Rock of masters, sons of rulers,
my beloved, slaves without owners.

Strengthen the hands of a poor people,
to be carefree in Zion,
my beloved, to sing songs accompanied by minstrels,
with pipes and lute, with joyous frivolities,
my beloved, to celebrate at festive seasons.
English translation by Sarah Grabiner

רָמָה יַד אוֹיְבִים וּמְעַנִּים,
זֶה כַּמָּה יָמִים וְשָׁנִים.
אֲהוּבִי, וְכִמְעַט שְׁנוֹת עוֹלָם פּוֹנִים.
אַיֵּה חֶזְיוֹנִים? נָמוּ נֶאֱמָנִים,
אֲהוּבִי, שׁוֹמֵר-אֱמוּנִים.

נִלְאֵיתִי נְשֹׂא עֹל מוֹנִים,
שָׂבַעְתִּי רַבַּת בִּזְיוֹנִים.
אֲהוּבִי, נָגְעָה חֶרֶב עַד גְּרוֹנִים
מַעֲרָב דּוֹדָנִים, מוֹאָבִים, עַמּוֹנִים,
אֲהוּבִי, אֱדוֹם וִיוָנִים.

פָּרְצוּ גָּדֵר וּבִנְיָנִים,
הָרְסוּ וְנָטְעוּ נַעֲמָנִים.
אֲהוּבִי, עָקְרוּ וְשָׁתְלוּ קִמְשׁוֹנִים.
אֵיךְ! צוּר גְּאוֹנִים, בְּנֵי אֲדוֹנִים,
אֲהוּבִי, עֲבָדִים וְאֵין קוֹנִים.

חַזֵּק יְדֵי עַם אֶבְיוֹנִים,
לִהְיוֹת בְּצִיּוֹן שַׁאֲנַנִּים,
אֲהוּבִי, לָשִׁיר שָׁרִים אַחַר נוֹגְנִים,
בְּעוּגָב וּמִינִים, בְּשִׂמְחוֹת שׁוֹשַׁנִּים,
אֲהוּבִי, וְלָחֹג בִּזְמַנִּים.

על אהבתך אשתה גביעי

AL AHAVATECHA ESHTEH G'VI-I

MUSIC: SHANI BEN-OR AND BOAZ DOROT
FROM KEHILLAT KOL HANESHAMA (JERUSALEM)
TEXT: YEHUDAH HALEVI (12TH C.)

עַל אַהֲבָתֵךְ אֶשְׁתֶּה גְבִיעִי:
שָׁלוֹם לָךְ, שָׁלוֹם יוֹם הַשְּׁבִיעִי.

To your love I raise my cup:
shalom, peace to you, my Seventh Day!

1. שֵׁשֶׁת יְמֵי מַעֲשֶׂה לָךְ כַּעֲבָדִים,
אִם אֶעֱבֹד בָּהֶם אֶשְׂבַּע נְדוּדִים.
כֻּלָּם בְּעֵינַי הֵם יָמִים אֲחָדִים,
מֵאַהֲבָתִי בָךְ, יוֹם שַׁעֲשׁוּעִי.

1. The six workdays enslaved to you,
even though I work, I wander aimlessly.
They seem to me to blur into one,
because of my love for you, day of enjoyment.

2. אֵצֵא בְיוֹם רִאשׁוֹן לַעֲשׂוֹת מְלָאכָה.
לַעֲרוֹךְ לְיוֹם שַׁבָּת הַמַּעֲרָכָה?
כִּי הָאֱלֹהִים שָׂם שָׁם הַבְּרָכָה.
אַתָּה לְבַד חֶלְקִי מִכָּל יְגִיעִי.

2. On the first day I set out on worker's path.
For whom else but you, Shabbat, do I prepare?
God who guides the heavens blesses you.
You alone are my portion, whatever I do.

3. מָאוֹר לְיוֹם קָדְשִׁי מֵאוֹר קְדוֹשִׁי,
שֶׁמֶשׁ וְכוֹכָבִים קִנְּאוּ לְשִׁמְשִׁי.
מַה לִּי לְיוֹם שֵׁנִי אוֹ לַשְּׁלִישִׁי?
יַסְתִּיר מְאוֹרוֹתָיו יוֹם הָרְבִיעִי.

3. Sacred light from sacred source,
sun and stars are jealous of Your light.
On the second and third days, what did I gain?
Hidden in darkness are the lights of the fourth day.

4. אֶשְׁמַע מְבַשֵּׂר טוֹב מִיּוֹם חֲמִישִׁי,
כִּי מָחֳרָת יִהְיֶה נֹפֶשׁ לְנַפְשִׁי.
בֹּקֶר לַעֲבוֹדוּתִי עֶרֶב לְחָפְשִׁי,
קָרוּא אֱלֵי שֻׁלְחַן מַלְכִּי וְרוֹעִי.

4. I hear the happy tidings of the fifth day,
for tomorrow will bring respite to my soul.
Morning in fetters, evening brings freedom's reign,
when my shepherd invites me to God's royal feast.

5. אֶמְצָא בְיוֹם שִׁשִּׁי נַפְשִׁי שְׂמֵחָה,
כִּי קָרְבָה אֵלַי עֵת הַמְּנוּחָה.
אִם נָע וָנָד אֵלֵךְ לִמְצֹא רְוָחָה,
עֶרֶב וְאֶשְׁכַּח כָּל נוֹדִי וְנוֹעִי.

5. On the sixth day my soul finds joy,
for the time of rest is drawing near.
I must wander restlessly to find all I need,
but this evening I shall forget all my restlessness.

6. מַה נָּעֲמָה לִי עֵת בֵּין הַשְּׁמָשׁוֹת,
לִרְאוֹת פְּנֵי שַׁבָּת פָּנִים חֲדָשׁוֹת.
בֹּאוּ בְתַפּוּחִים הַרְבּוּ אֲשִׁישׁוֹת,
זֶה יוֹם מְנוּחִי, זֶה דוֹדִי וְרֵעִי.

6. Yes, delicious is to me this twilight time,
to behold the renewed face of Shabbat.
Approach with apples, come with sweets,
on my day of rest, my friend, my beloved.

עם אחד

AM ECHAD

MUSIC AND TEXT: ARIEL ZURAYEV, YEHUDA KAPLAN, AND YONATAN GIRTZ
"HATIKVAH" TEXT EXCERPT BY NAFTALI HERZ IMBER

G
C
Bm
Sh'ma Yis-ra-el__ om-rim__ yach-dav.__ Od lo av-dah tik-va-tei-nu
Gmaj7
D
1.
lih'-yot chof-shi b'-ar-tzei-nu. Sh'ma Yis-ra-el,__ ku-la-nu am e-chad.
A(add9)
2.
A(add9)
[optional rap section]
la-nu am e-chad.__ Am e-
D
Bm
Gmaj7
D
chad,__ am e-chad,__ am e-chad, ku-la-nu am e-chad.
A
E
Bm
Gmaj7
Am e-chad,__ am e-chad,__
optional second voice
Od lo av-dah tik-va-tei-nu lih'-yot chof-shi
D
rit.
A
__ am e-chad, ku-la-nu am e-chad.__
b'-ar-tzei-nu, sh'ma Yis-ra-el,__ ku-la-nu am e-chad.__

Without words, without feelings,
there is no escape from thoughts.
There is an unexplained tear here.
How can we sing when the heart is broken?

I'm here in front of the news,
I cannot digest the tears.
If we are a chosen people,
how a cruel fate was carved.

And there are no answers.
A heavy fog has now descended.
Who do you reach out to?
The soul is wounded in battle.
(*"Sh'ma,"* Israel is saying together.)

Our hope is not lost yet
to be free in our country.
Sh'ma Israel; we are all one nation.

Our hope is not lost...

לְלֹא מִלִּים, לְלֹא תְּחוּשׁוֹת,
אֵין מָנוֹס מִמַּחֲשָׁבוֹת.
יֵשׁ פֹּה קֶרַע לֹא מֻסְבָּר.
אֵיךְ שָׁרִים כְּשֶׁהַלֵּב נִשְׁבָּר?

אֲנִי פֹּה מוּל הַחֲדָשׁוֹת,
לֹא מְעַכֵּל אֶת הַדְּמָעוֹת.
אִם אֲנַחְנוּ עַם נִבְחָר,
אֵיךְ נֶחְרַט גּוֹרָל אַכְזָר.

וְאֵין תְּשׁוּבוֹת.
עֲרָפֶל כָּבֵד נָחַת עַכְשָׁיו.
לְמִי פּוֹנִים?
הַנְּשָׁמָה פְּצוּעָה בַּקְּרָב.
(שְׁמַע יִשְׂרָאֵל אוֹמְרִים יַחְדָּיו.)

עוֹד לֹא אָבְדָה תִּקְוָתֵנוּ
לִהְיוֹת חָפְשִׁי בְּאַרְצֵנוּ.
שְׁמַע יִשְׂרָאֵל, כֻּלָּנוּ עַם אֶחָד.

תִּקְוָתֵנוּ...

Optional rap

The horrors cannot be described in words.
The soul is wounded; we just wanted to dance.
Don't want to see crying mothers anymore.
What do we have to do to live in a quiet peace?

אִי אֶפְשָׁר לְתָאֵר בַּמִּלִּים תַּ'זְוָעוֹת.
הַנֶּפֶשׁ פְּצוּעָה; רַק רָצִינוּ לִרְקֹד.
לֹא רוֹצִים עוֹד לִרְאוֹת אִמָּהוֹת שֶׁבּוֹכוֹת.
מָה כְּבָר בִּקַּשְׁנוּ בְּשֶׁקֶט לִחְיוֹת?

We have no other country
even if the ground here is on fire.
So enough of the division, enough of the hatred.
They look at us and take advantage of a weakness.

אֵין לָנוּ אֶרֶץ אַחֶרֶת (אַחֶרֶת)
גַּם אִם הָאֲדָמָה פֹּה בּוֹעֶרֶת.
אָז דַּי לַפִּלּוּג, דַּי לְשִׂנְאָה .
מִסְתַּכְּלִים עָלֵינוּ, מְנַצְּלִים תַּ'חֻלְשָׁה.

This is the time to love and spread hope.
Raise your head and smile back
because we are all brothers not only in war.
The people of Israel are family.

זֶה הַזְּמַן לֶאֱהֹב לְהָפִיץ תַּ'תִּקְוָה.
לְהָרִים אֶת הָרֹאשׁ, לְחַיֵּךְ חֲזָרָה
כִּי כֻּלָּנוּ אַחִים, לֹא רַק בַּמִּלְחָמָה.
עַם יִשְׂרָאֵל זוֹ אוֹתָהּ מִשְׁפָּחָה.

We will win; there are no doubts.
In history, we won all the battles.
And to all the haters: Yalla bye!
Israel lives!

אֲנַחְנוּ נְנַצֵּחַ, אֵין פֹּה סְפֵקוֹת.
בַּהִסְטוֹרְיָה נִצַּחְנוּ בְּכָל הַקְּרָבוֹת.
כָּל הַשּׂוֹנְאִים יַאלְלָה בַּיי!
עַם יִשְׂרָאֵל חַי!

בכל דור ודור

B'CHOL DOR VADOR

MUSIC: MORDECHAI CORCOS
AS SUNG AT KIBBUTZ NEOT SEMADAR
TEXT: PASSOVER HAGGADAH

As in every age and generation,
the task is ours:
to see ourselves as if we had come out of Egypt.

בְּכָל דּוֹר וָדוֹר
חַיָּב אָדָם לִרְאוֹת אֶת עַצְמוֹ
כְּאִלּוּ הוּא יָצָא מִמִּצְרָיִם.

אל אדון

EIL ADON

MUSIC: RUTI SOKOLOFF
TEXT: LITURGY

God, master of all existence,
praised by all that breathes,
the world is filled with Your greatness and glory;
knowledge and understanding surround You.

אֵל אָדוֹן עַל כָּל הַמַּעֲשִׂים,
בָּרוּךְ וּמְבֹרָךְ בְּפִי כָּל נְשָׁמָה,
גָּדְלוֹ וְטוּבוֹ מָלֵא עוֹלָם,
דַּעַת וּתְבוּנָה סוֹבְבִים אוֹתוֹ.

Exalted above holy beings,
resplendent in glory on Your chariot,
integrity and mercy stand before Your throne,
love and merit accompany Your presence.

הַמִּתְגָּאֶה עַל חַיּוֹת הַקֹּדֶשׁ,
וְנֶהְדָּר בְּכָבוֹד עַל הַמֶּרְכָּבָה,
זְכוּת וּמִישׁוֹר לִפְנֵי כִסְאוֹ,
חֶסֶד וְרַחֲמִים לִפְנֵי כְבוֹדוֹ.

הללויה

HAL'LUYAH (PSALM 150)

MUSIC: DAPHNA ROSENBERG
FROM NAVA TEHILA (JERUSALEM)
TEXT: PSALM 150

F E Dm E Dm E Dm F
B♭ A Gm A Gm A Gm B♭
27
ha - l' - lu Yah! Ha - l' - lu Yah, ha - l' - lu Yah, ha - l' - lu
E
A
32
Last time to Coda
D.C. al Coda
Yah!
CODA
Am Dm F E Am
Dm Gm B♭ A Dm
34
Kol ha - n - sha - mah t' - ha - leil Yah l' - lu Yah, kol ha - n - sha -
Dm F E E Dm E Dm
Gm B♭ A A Gm A Gm
39
C
mah t' - ha - leil Yah l' - lu Yah. Ha - l' - lu Yah, ha - l' - lu Yah,
F E Dm E Dm E Dm F
B♭ A Gm A Gm A Gm B♭
44
ha - l' - lu Yah! Ha - l' - lu Yah, ha - l' - lu Yah, ha - l' - lu
E Dm E Dm E Dm F E Dm E Dm
A Gm A Gm A Gm B♭ A Gm A Gm
49
Yah! Ha-l'-lu Yah, ha-l'-lu Yah, ha - l' - lu Yah! Ha-l'-lu Yah,
E Dm F E
A Gm B♭ A
55
ha - l' - lu Yah, ha - l' - lu Yah!

Hallelujah!	הַלְלוּ יָהּ!
Praise God in God's sanctuary;	הַלְלוּ־אֵל בְּקָדְשׁוֹ,
praise God in the sky, God's stronghold.	הַלְלוּהוּ בִּרְקִיעַ עֻזּוֹ.
Praise God for mighty acts;	הַלְלוּהוּ בִגְבוּרֹתָיו,
praise God for God's exceeding greatness.	הַלְלוּהוּ כְּרֹב גֻּדְלוֹ.
Praise God with blasts of the horn;	הַלְלוּהוּ בְּתֵקַע שׁוֹפָר,
praise God with harp and lyre.	הַלְלוּהוּ בְּנֵבֶל וְכִנּוֹר.
Praise God with timbrel and dance;	הַלְלוּהוּ בְתֹף וּמָחוֹל,
praise God with lute and pipe.	הַלְלוּהוּ בְּמִנִּים וְעוּגָב.
Praise God with resounding cymbals;	הַלְלוּהוּ בְצִלְצְלֵי־שָׁמַע,
praise God with loud-clashing cymbals.	הַלְלוּהוּ בְּצִלְצְלֵי־תְרוּעָה.
Let all that breathes praise God.	כֹּל הַנְּשָׁמָה תְּהַלֵּל יָהּ,
Hallelujah!	הַלְלוּ־יָהּ!

הנרות

HaneiRot

MUSIC: VERED IVTSAN
TEXT: AVITAL BEN-CHORIN / LITURGY, ED. GOLAN BEN-CHORIN

In Jerusalem of the 1950s, Avital Ben-Chorin, *z"l*, a young woman who fled Nazi Germany alone as a thirteen-year-old, lit Shabbat candles in her newfound home. As a meticulous linguist and honest thinker, and later a founder of the first Israeli Reform congregation, Kehilat Har-El (Jerusalem), she understood the act of lighting Shabbat candles as a human expression of holiness rather than a divine commandment, which actually does not appear in the Torah. Consequently, she wrote an original blessing: "May these candles be a manifestation of blessing on your holy Shabbat as they cast upon us Shabbat's delight." In keeping with the Reform ideal of tradition and innovation, her words were edited by her husband Schalom and their son Tovia. The words were printed in the first Israeli Reform siddur, *HaAvodah SheBaLev*. Today, they accompany the lighting of Shabbat candles in many Israeli Reform synagogues and homes. *—Rabbi Golan Ben-Chorin Ed.D.*

May these candles be a manifestation
of blessing on Your holy Shabbat
as they cast upon us Shabbat's delight.
Enlighten our eyes with Your Torah,
focus our minds on Your mitzvot,
unite our hearts in love and reverence
for Your name.
Extend Your light upon us
and Your peace upon all who dwell on earth.

יִהְיוּ הַנֵּרוֹת הַלָּלוּ
אוֹת בְּרָכָה בְּשַׁבָּת קָדְשְׁךָ
וְיַשְׁרוּ עָלֵינוּ חֶדְוַת שַׁבָּת.
הָאֵר עֵינֵינוּ בְּתוֹרָתֶךָ,
וְדַבֵּק לִבֵּנוּ בְּמִצְוֹתֶיךָ,
וְיַחֵד לְבָבֵנוּ לְאַהֲבָה וּלְיִרְאָה
אֶת שְׁמֶךָ.
שְׁלַח אוֹרְךָ עָלֵינוּ
וּשְׁלוֹמְךָ עַל כָּל יוֹשְׁבֵי תֵּבֵל.

האור מציון

HAOR MITZIYON

MUSIC AND TEXT: KALEY HALPERIN

Building in intensity ♩ = 88

הִנֵּה עוֹלֶה הָאוֹר מִצִּיּוֹן,
זוֹרֵחַ וּבָא בִּשְׁלַל צִבְעֵי הַקֶּשֶׁת.
מְנַשֵּׁק וּמְרַפֵּא מֵעֵבֶר לַדִּמְיוֹן;
הִנֵּה עוֹלֶה הָאוֹר מִצִּיּוֹן.

Here comes the light from Zion,
rises and comes in all colors of the rainbow.
Kisses and hugs—more than can be imagined;
here comes the light from Zion.

כי אשמרה שבת | ושמרו

KI ESHM'RAH SHABBAT / V'SHAM'RU

MUSIC: TRADITIONAL MOROCCAN
TEXT: ABRAHAM IBN EZRA (11TH C.)

When I keep Shabbat, God keeps me.
It is a sign forever between God and me.

It is forbidden to do regular things,
discussing only what is necessary,
not words of business, not even words of politics.
Studying God's Torah will make me wise.

כִּי אֶשְׁמְרָה שַׁבָּת אֵל יִשְׁמְרֵנִי.
אוֹת הִיא לְעוֹלְמֵי עַד בֵּינוֹ וּבֵינִי.

אָסוּר מְצֹא חֵפֶץ לַעֲשׂוֹת דְּרָכִים,
גַּם מִלְּדַבֵּר בּוֹ דִּבְרֵי צְרָכִים,
דִּבְרֵי סְחוֹרָה אוֹ דִּבְרֵי מְלָכִים.
אֶהְגֶּה בְּתוֹרַת אֵל וּתְחַכְּמֵנִי.

V'SHAM'RU

MUSIC: TRADITIONAL MOROCCAN, "KI ESHM'RAH SHABBAT" MELODY
AS SUNG AT KEHILLAT YOZMA (MODI'IN) ED. BE'AYIN MIZRACHIT
TEXT: SHABBAT LITURGY

V'SHAM'RU ושמרו

The people of Israel shall keep Shabbat,	וְשָׁמְרוּ בְנֵי יִשְׂרָאֵל אֶת הַשַּׁבָּת,
observing Shabbat throughout the ages	לַעֲשׂוֹת אֶת הַשַּׁבָּת לְדֹרֹתָם
as a covenant for all time.	בְּרִית עוֹלָם.
It is a sign for all time	בֵּינִי וּבֵין בְּנֵי יִשְׂרָאֵל
between Me and the people of Israel,	אוֹת הִיא לְעוֹלָם,
for in six days Adonai	כִּי־שֵׁשֶׁת יָמִים עָשָׂה יְיָ
made heaven and earth,	אֶת־הַשָּׁמַיִם וְאֶת־הָאָרֶץ,
and on the seventh day God ceased from work and was refreshed.	וּבַיּוֹם הַשְּׁבִיעִי שָׁבַת וַיִּנָּפַשׁ.

כי שמחתני

KI SIMACHTANI

MUSIC: DAPHNA ROSENBERG AND RUTH GAN KAGAN
FROM NAVA TEHILA (JERUSALEM)
TEXT: PSALM 92:5

You have gladdened me by Your deeds, Yah;
I shout for joy at Your handiwork.

כִּי שִׂמַּחְתַּנִי יָהּ בְּפׇעֳלֶךָ
בְּמַעֲשֵׂי יָדֶיךָ אֲרַנֵּן.

קריה יפהפיה

KIRYAH Y'FEIHFIYAH

MUSIC: MAUREEN NEHEDAR
TEXT: ZECHARIAH AL DHAHIRI ("KIRYAH Y'FEIHFIYAH") (16TH C.)
AND YEHUDAH HALEVI ("Y'FEIH NOF M'SOS TEIVEIL") (11TH C.)

* This edition omits an additional repetition of the "Umi yitneini..." verse, included in Nehedar's original recording, which contains a modulation to an instrumental section.

קְרְיָה יְפֵהפִיָּה מָשׂוֹשׂ לְעָרֵיךָ,
לָךְ נִכְסְפָה נַפְשִׁי מִפַּאֲתֵי מַעְרָב.
הֲמוֹן רַחֲמַי נִכְמָר כִּי אֶזְכְּרָה קֶדֶם,
כְּבוֹדֵךְ אֲשֶׁר גָּלָה וְנָוֵךְ אֲשֶׁר חָרַב.

City of splendor, crown jewel of Your towns,
my soul yearns for you from the edge of the west.
I am overcome with compassion, as I remember
your formerly-shining glory, your beauty which was destroyed.

יְפֵה נוֹף מְשׂוֹשׂ תֵּבֵל קִרְיָה לְמֶלֶךְ רָב,
לָךְ נִכְסְפָה נַפְשִׁי מִפַּאֲתֵי מַעְרָב.
יוֹם אֶזְכְּרָה יִפְעַת רַבַּת צְבָאַיִךְ,
וְטַעַם רְגָבַיִךְ לִי יֶעְרַב.

The beauty of the vista, earth's delight, the city of a great king,
my soul yearns for you from the edge of the west.
Someday may I recall the magnificence of your great troops,
and may the taste of the dust of your earth bring me sweetness.

וּמִי יִתְּנֵנִי עַל כַּנְפֵי נְשָׁרִים
עַד אֲרַוֶּה בְדִמְעָתִי עֲפָרֵךְ וְיִתְעָרָב.

If only I could reach you on eagles' wings
so that I could quench your dust with my tears, mingling together.

דְּרַשְׁתִּיךְ. וְאִם מַלְכֵּךְ אֵין בָּךְ,
וְאִם בִּמְקוֹם
צְרִי גִלְעָדֵךְ נָחָשׁ שָׂרָף וְגַם עַקְרָב,
הֲלֹא אֶת אֲבָנַיִךְ אֲחוֹנֵן וְאֶשָּׁקֵם?
וְטַעַם רְגָבַיִךְ לְפִי מִדְּבַשׁ יֶעְרַב.

I seek you. But if your king is not there with you,
if instead of a soothing balm,
there are serpents, vipers, and scorpions,
might I just bring some grace to your stones, might I kiss them?
The taste of your dusty earth will be sweeter to me than honey.
English translation by Sarah Grabiner

כל חמירא

KOL CHAMIRA

MUSIC: KALEY HALPERIN
TEXT: BLESSING FOR THE BURNING OF CHAMEITZ, AD. KALEY HALPERIN

All *chameitz* that is in my responsibility,	כָּל חֲמִירָא וַחֲמִיעָא שֶׁבִּרְשׁוּתִי,
that is not in my responsibility,	דְּלָא בִּרְשׁוּתִי,
will be like the dirt of the land.	יִהְיֶה כְּעָפָר דְּאַרְצָא.
That which I have seen, that which I have not seen.	דַּרְאִיתֵיה דְּלָא רְאִיתֵיה,
That which I have witnessed, that which I have not witnessed.	דַּחֲזִיתֵהּ דְּלָא חֲזִיתֵהּ,
That which I have seen.	דַּרְאִיתֵיה.

למדני

LAMDEINI

MUSIC: MAYA RAVIV
TEXT: PSALM 143:10-12

CODA

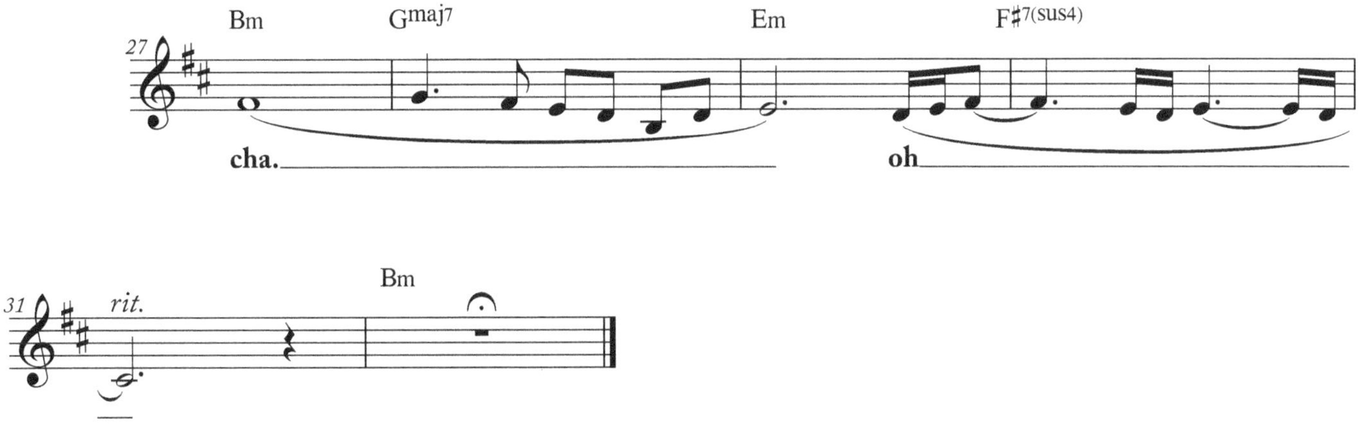

Teach me to do Your will,
for You are my God;
may Your good Spirit
lead me on level ground.
For Your name's sake, God, preserve my life;
in Your righteousness, bring me out of trouble.
In Your unfailing love, silence my enemies;
destroy all my foes,
for I am Your servant.

לַמְּדֵנִי לַעֲשׂוֹת רְצוֹנֶךָ
כִּי־אַתָּה אֱלוֹהָי
רוּחֲךָ טוֹבָה
תַּנְחֵנִי בְּאֶרֶץ מִישׁוֹר.
לְמַעַן־שִׁמְךָ יְיָ תְּחַיֵּנִי
בְּצִדְקָתְךָ תוֹצִיא מִצָּרָה נַפְשִׁי
וּבְחַסְדְּךָ תַּצְמִית אֹיְבָי
וְהַאֲבַדְתָּ כָּל־צֹרְרֵי נַפְשִׁי
כִּי אֲנִי עַבְדֶּךָ.

למדני

LAMDEINI

MUSIC: YONATAN TOKAYER
AS SUNG BY YONINA
TEXT: LEAH GOLDBERG

 994070

Teach me, O God, a blessing, a prayer
on the mystery of a withered leaf,
on ripened fruit so fair,
on the freedom to see, to sense,
to breathe, to know,
to hope, to despair.

לַמְּדֵנִי, אֱלֹהַי, בָּרֵךְ וְהִתְפַּלֵּל
עַל סוֹד עָלֶה קָמֵל,
עַל נֹגַהּ פְּרִי בָּשֵׁל,
עַל הַחֵרוּת הַזֹּאת:
לִרְאוֹת, לָחוּשׁ, לִנְשֹׁם,
לָדַעַת, לְיַחֵל, לְהִכָּשֵׁל.

Teach my lips a blessing,
a hymn of praise,
as each morning
and night
You renew Your days,
lest my days be today as the one before;
lest routine set my ways.

לַמֵּד אֶת שִׂפְתוֹתַי
בְּרָכָה וְשִׁיר הַלֵּל,
בְּהִתְחַדֵּשׁ זְמַנְּךָ
עִם בֹּקֶר וְעִם לֵיל,
לְבַל יִהְיֶה יוֹמִי הַיּוֹם
כִּתְמוֹל שִׁלְשׁוֹם,
לְבַל יִהְיֶה עָלַי יוֹמִי הֶרְגֵּל.

לכה דודי

L'CHAH DODI

MUSIC: MAUREEN NEHEDAR
TEXT: SHLOMO ALKABETZ BEN HALEVI (16TH C.)

CODA
VERSES 5, 6, & 9
G D Em
lah. 5. Hit - o - r' - ri, hit-o - r' - ri, ki va_ o-
(6.) shi v'-lo ti - ka - mi, mah tish - to-
(9.) lom a - te-ret ba - lah, gam b' - sim-
G D G D
reich, ku-mi o - ri, u - ri u - ri shir da - bei-
cha - chi u - mah te - he - mi, bach ye - che - su a - ni - yei a -
chah uv-tzo - ho - lah, toch e - mu - nei am s' - gu -
Em 1. G D G
ri, k'vod A - do - nai a - la-yich nig - lah. 6. Lo tei - vo-
mi, v' - niv - n' - optional: 9. Bo - i v'-sha-
lah, bo - i cha-
2. G FINAL CHORUS D
tah ir al ti - lah. L'-chah do - di lik-rat ka-
lah, bo - i cha - lah.
A Em G
lah, p'-nei Shab - bat n'-ka - b' - lah. L'-chah do-
Bm A Em
di lik-rat ka - lah, p'-nei Shab - bat n'-ka - b'-
G END D A
rit.
lah. L'-chah do - di lik-rat ka - lah. Bo-i cha-
Em G D
lah, Shab-bat ha-Mal - kah.

Beloved, come to meet the bride;
beloved, come to greet Shabbat.

לְכָה דוֹדִי לִקְרַאת כַּלָּה,
פְּנֵי שַׁבָּת נְקַבְּלָה.

1. "Keep" and "remember": a single command
the Only God caused us to hear;
the Eternal is One, God's name is One;
glory and praise are God's.

1. שָׁמוֹר וְזָכוֹר בְּדִבּוּר אֶחָד,
הִשְׁמִיעָנוּ אֵל הַמְיֻחָד,
יְיָ אֶחָד וּשְׁמוֹ אֶחָד,
לְשֵׁם וּלְתִפְאֶרֶת וְלִתְהִלָּה.

2. Come with me to meet Shabbat,
forever a fountain of blessing.
Still it flows, as from the start:
the last of days, for which the first was made.

2. לִקְרַאת שַׁבָּת לְכוּ וְנֵלְכָה,
כִּי הִיא מְקוֹר הַבְּרָכָה,
מֵרֹאשׁ מִקֶּדֶם נְסוּכָה,
סוֹף מַעֲשֶׂה בְּמַחֲשָׁבָה תְּחִלָּה.

5. Awake, awake,
your light has come!
Arise, shine, awake, and sing:
the Eternal's glory dawns upon you.

5. הִתְעוֹרְרִי, הִתְעוֹרְרִי,
כִּי בָא אוֹרֵךְ, קוּמִי אוֹרִי,
עוּרִי עוּרִי, שִׁיר דַּבֵּרִי,
כְּבוֹד יְיָ עָלַיִךְ נִגְלָה.

6. An end to shame and degradation;
forget your sorrow; quiet your groans.
The afflicted of my people find respite in you,
the city renewed upon its ancient ruins.

6. לֹא תֵבוֹשִׁי וְלֹא תִכָּלְמִי,
מַה תִּשְׁתּוֹחֲחִי וּמַה תֶּהֱמִי,
בָּךְ יֶחֱסוּ עֲנִיֵּי עַמִּי,
וְנִבְנְתָה עִיר עַל תִּלָּהּ.

9. Enter in peace, O crown of your husband;
enter in gladness, enter in joy.
Come to the people that keeps its faith.
Enter, O bride! Enter, O bride!

9. בּוֹאִי בְשָׁלוֹם עֲטֶרֶת בַּעְלָהּ,
גַּם בְּשִׂמְחָה וּבְצָהֳלָה,
תּוֹךְ אֱמוּנֵי עַם סְגֻלָּה,
בּוֹאִי כַלָּה, בּוֹאִי כַלָּה.

Enter, O bride, O Sabbath queen.

בּוֹאִי כַלָּה, שַׁבָּת הַמַּלְכָּה.

לכה דודי

L'CHAH DODI

MUSIC: TRADITIONAL SEPHARDIC (Y'RUSHALMI)
AS SUNG AT KEHILLAT YOZMA (MODI'IN) ED. BE'AYIN MIZRACHIT
TEXT: SHLOMO ALKABETZ BEN HALEVI (16TH C.)

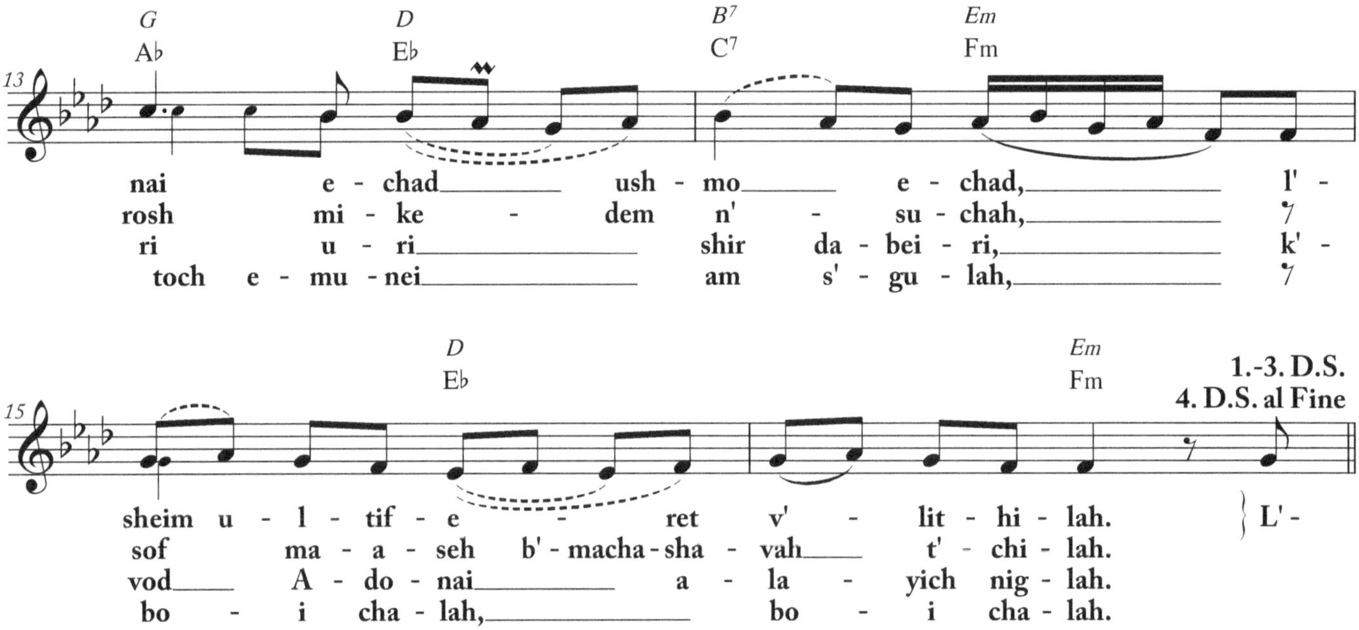

Beloved, come to meet the bride;
beloved, come to greet Shabbat.

לְכָה דוֹדִי לִקְרַאת כַּלָּה,
פְּנֵי שַׁבָּת נְקַבְּלָה.

1. "Keep" and "remember": a single command
the Only God caused us to hear;
the Eternal is One, God's name is One;
glory and praise are God's.

1. שָׁמוֹר וְזָכוֹר בְּדִבּוּר אֶחָד,
הִשְׁמִיעָנוּ אֵל הַמְיֻחָד,
יְיָ אֶחָד וּשְׁמוֹ אֶחָד,
לְשֵׁם וּלְתִפְאֶרֶת וְלִתְהִלָּה.

2. Come with me to meet Shabbat,
forever a fountain of blessing.
Still it flows, as from the start:
the last of days, for which the first was made.

2. לִקְרַאת שַׁבָּת לְכוּ וְנֵלְכָה,
כִּי הִיא מְקוֹר הַבְּרָכָה,
מֵרֹאשׁ מִקֶּדֶם נְסוּכָה,
סוֹף מַעֲשֶׂה בְּמַחֲשָׁבָה תְּחִלָּה.

5. Awake, awake,
your light has come!
Arise, shine, awake, and sing:
the Eternal's glory dawns upon you.

5. הִתְעוֹרְרִי, הִתְעוֹרְרִי,
כִּי בָא אוֹרֵךְ, קוּמִי אוֹרִי,
עוּרִי עוּרִי, שִׁיר דַּבֵּרִי,
כְּבוֹד יְיָ עָלַיִךְ נִגְלָה.

9. Enter in peace, O crown of your husband;
enter in gladness, enter in joy.
Come to the people that keeps its faith.
Enter, O bride! Enter, O bride!

9. בּוֹאִי בְשָׁלוֹם עֲטֶרֶת בַּעְלָהּ,
גַּם בְּשִׂמְחָה וּבְצָהֳלָה,
תּוֹךְ אֱמוּנֵי עַם סְגֻלָּה,
בּוֹאִי כַלָּה, בּוֹאִי כַלָּה.

לאל עורך דין

L'EIL OREICH DIN

MUSIC AND FEMININE TEXT: DAPHNA ROSENBERG AND RUTH GAN KAGAN
FROM NAVA TEHILA (JERUSALEM)
TEXT: ROSH HASHANAH LITURGY
AD. DAPHNA ROSENBERG AND RUTH GAN KAGAN

31
B7 Em Cmaj7 B7 Em
C♯7 F♯m Dmaj7 C♯7 F♯m
b' - Yom Din. L'-ta-heir cho - se - ha ba-din.
cho - sav
36
B
Em Cmaj7 Em
F♯m Dmaj7 F♯m
L'-yo-dei - a ma-cha-sha-vot b'-Yom Din.
40
B7 Em Cmaj7 G B7
C♯7 F♯m Dmaj7 A C♯7
L'-cho-veish ka-a-so ba - din. L'-lo-ve-
L'-lo-veish
45
C G B7 Em Cmaj7
D A C♯7 F♯m Dmaj7
- shet tz' - da-kot b'-Yom Din. L'-mo-che - let a - vo-not
L'-mo-cheil
50
B7 Em Am7 B7
C♯7 F♯m Bm7 C♯7
ba - din. L'-no-ra t' - hi-lot b' - Yom Din.
55
Em Am7 D7 G
F♯m Bm7 E7 A
L'-so-lei - ach la-a-mu-sav ba-din.
60
B7 C G B7 Em
C♯7 D A C♯7 F♯m
L'-o-nah l'-kor-e - ha b'-Yom Din. L'-fo-e-
L'-o-neh l'-kor - av L'-fo-eil

Cmaj7 Dmaj7 B7 C#7 Em F#m C Em F#m
65
- let ra - cha - me - ha ba-din. L'-tzo-feh nis-ta-rot
ra - cha-mav
Cmaj7 Dmaj7 Em F#m B7 C#7 Em F#m Cmaj7 Dmaj7
70
b'-Yom Din. L'-ko-neh a-va-dav ba - din.
G A B7 C#7 C D G A B7 C#7
75
L' - ra-cheim a-mah b' - Yom Din.
a - mo
Em F#m Cmaj7 Dmaj7 B7 C#7 Em F#m
80
L'-sho - me - ret o - ha-vei - ha ba-din. L'-to-meich
L'-sho-meir o - ha-vav
C D G A B7 C#7 Em F#m Cmaj7 Dmaj7
85
t' - mi-mav b' - Yom Din. Mmm mmm
B7 C#7 Em F#m
90
mmm

To the ultimate arbiter of justice,
who probes all hearts on the Day of Judgment
and reveals what is hidden, with justice;
who is the voice of truth on the Day of Judgment
and pronounces rules of justice;
who is wise and acts lovingly on the Day of Judgment
and remembers the covenant, while dispensing justice;
who has compassion for all creation on the Day of Judgment
and purifies the faithful with justice;
who knows our thoughts on the Day of Judgment
and overcomes anger with justice;
who is clothed in righteousness on the Day of Judgment
and whose forgiveness of wrongdoing is a hallmark of justice;
who is revered in praises on the Day of Judgment
and exonerates us as an exercise of justice;
who responds to those who cry out on the Day of Judgment
and demonstrates mercy in justice;
who discerns all mysteries on the Day of Judgment
and holds close those who serve God with justice;
who has compassion for the people Israel on the Day of Judgment
and guards those who love God, with justice;
and who upholds those who trust wholeheartedly in the Divine
on the Day of Judgment.

לְאֵל עוֹרֵךְ דִּין.
לְבוֹחֵן לְבָבוֹת בְּיוֹם דִּין.
לְגוֹלֶה עֲמוּקוֹת בַּדִּין.
לְדוֹבֶרֶת (לְדוֹבֵר) מֵישָׁרִים בְּיוֹם דִּין.
לְהוֹגָה (לְהוֹגֶה) דֵעוֹת בַּדִּין.
לְוָתִיק וְעֹשֶׂה חֶסֶד בְּיוֹם דִּין.
לְזוֹכֵר בְּרִיתוֹ בַּדִּין.
לְחוֹמֶלֶת (לְחוֹמֵל) מַעֲשֶׂיהָ (מַעֲשָׂיו) בְּיוֹם דִּין.
לְטַהֵר חוֹסֶיהָ (חוֹסָיו) בַּדִּין.
לְיוֹדֵעַ מַחֲשָׁבוֹת בְּיוֹם דִּין.
לְכוֹבֵשׁ כַּעֲסוֹ בַּדִּין.
לְלוֹבֶשֶׁת (לְלוֹבֵשׁ) צְדָקוֹת בְּיוֹם דִּין.
לְמוֹחֶלֶת (לְמוֹחֵל) עֲוֹנוֹת בַּדִּין.
לְנוֹרָא תְהִלּוֹת בְּיוֹם דִּין.
לְסוֹלֵחַ לַעֲמוּסָיו בַּדִּין.
לְעוֹנָה (לְעוֹנֶה) לְקוֹרְאֶיהָ (לְקוֹרְאָיו) בְּיוֹם דִּין.
לְפוֹעֶלֶת (לְפוֹעֵל) רַחֲמֶיהָ (רַחֲמָיו) בַּדִּין.
לְצוֹפֶה נִסְתָּרוֹת בְּיוֹם דִּין.
לְקוֹנֶה עֲבָדָיו בַּדִּין.
לְרַחֵם עַמָּהּ (עַמּוֹ) בְּיוֹם דִּין.
לְשׁוֹמֶרֶת (לְשׁוֹמֵר) אוֹהֲבֶיהָ (אוֹהֲבָיו) בַּדִּין.
לְתוֹמֵךְ תְּמִימָיו
בְּיוֹם דִּין.

לא ישא גוי

LO YISA GOI

MUSIC: DAPHNA ROSENBERG AND YOEL SYKES
FROM NAVA TEHILA (JERUSALEM)
TEXT: ISAIAH 2:4-5, ZECHARIAH 8:19,
AD. DAPHNA ROSENBERG AND YOEL SYKES

Nation shall not take up sword against nation;
they shall never again study war.

לֹא־יִשָּׂא גוֹי אֶל־גּוֹי חֶרֶב,
וְלֹא־יִלְמְדוּ עוֹד מִלְחָמָה.

Come, let us walk by the light of God.

לְכוּ וְנֵלְכָה בְּאוֹר הֲוָיָה.

You must love honesty and integrity.

וְהָאֱמֶת וְהַשָּׁלוֹם, אֱהָבוּ.

מה נאוו עלי

MAH NAVU ALEI

MUSIC: TRADITIONAL IRAQI
ED. YAHALA LACHMISH/TANDU
TEXT: SHIMON BAR NISIM (20TH C.)

1. How pleasant atop the mountains are the footsteps
of the messenger bearing tidings of peace in your city.
The voices of your watchmen will rise up in joy;
shake off your sorrow,
your eyes shall behold the Sh'chinah
and your sons shall return to your borders.

1. מַה נָּאווּ עֲלֵי הֶהָרִים רַגְלֵי
מְבַשֵּׂר שָׁלוֹם בְּבִנְיַן עִירֵךְ.
קוֹל צוֹפַיִךְ יִשְׂאוּ קוֹל רִנָּה,
הִתְנַעֲרִי מִתּוֹךְ מְגִנָּה,
עַיִן בְּעַיִן תִּרְאִי שְׁכִינָה
וְשָׁבוּ בָנַיִךְ לִגְבוּלֵךְ.

2. Freedom to the captives in song and melody,
to the Temple may your path lead.
Pave, pave the pathway,
break forth in delight and glory.
A messenger will come with a word on his tongue.
Arise and shine, for your light has come.

2. לִשְׁבוּיִים דְּרוֹר בְּשִׁיר וּמִזְמוֹר,
אֶל בֵּית הַר הַמּוֹר יְהִי שְׁבִילֵךְ.
סֹלּוּ סֹלּוּ אֶת הַמְסִלָּה,
פִּצְחוּ רְנָנָה וּתְהִלָּה.
יָבֹא מְבַשֵּׂר בִּלְשׁוֹנוֹ מִלָּה.
קוּמִי עוּרִי כִּי בָא אוֹרֵךְ.

3. Leave Babylon where they worship Beil;
the harp and lyre will accompany your song.
Greatly rejoice, all mourners, in Zion;
come take refuge in the shadow of the Most High.
I shall build for you a magnificent palace.
I shall set a throne for your king, David.

3. צְאִי מִבָּבֶל קִרְיַת עוֹבְדֵי בֵל,
כִּנּוֹר וָנֵבֶל אָז יְהִי שִׁירֵךְ.
שׂוֹשׂ יָשִׂישׂוּ כָּל אֲבֵלֵי צִיּוֹן,
לָבֹא לַחֲסוֹת בְּצֵל הָעֶלְיוֹן.
בָּנֹה אֶבְנֶה לָךְ נְוֵה אַפִּרְיוֹן.
אָכִין כִּסֵּא לְדָוִד מַלְכֵּךְ.

4. Lift your eyes and see your children;
they have come to you, to the light in your light.
In place of darkness I will give you light;
then from Zion, Torah shall come forth.
For it will be great and awful
on the day you shall place a crown upon your head.

4. שְׂאִי עֵינַיִךְ וּרְאִי בָנַיִךְ,
בָּאוּ אֵלַיִךְ לָאוֹר בְּאוֹרֵךְ.
תַּחַת חֹשֶׁךְ אָשִׂים לָךְ אוֹרָה,
אָז מִצִּיּוֹן תֵּצֵא הַתּוֹרָה.
הִנֵּה גָּדוֹל הוּא אָיֹם וְנוֹרָא
בְּיוֹם שִׂימִי כֶּתֶר לְרֹאשֵׁךְ.

מה־טבו

MAH TOVU

MUSIC: BARUCH SHIRYON
FROM KEHILLAT YOZMA (MODI'IN)
TEXT: LITURGY

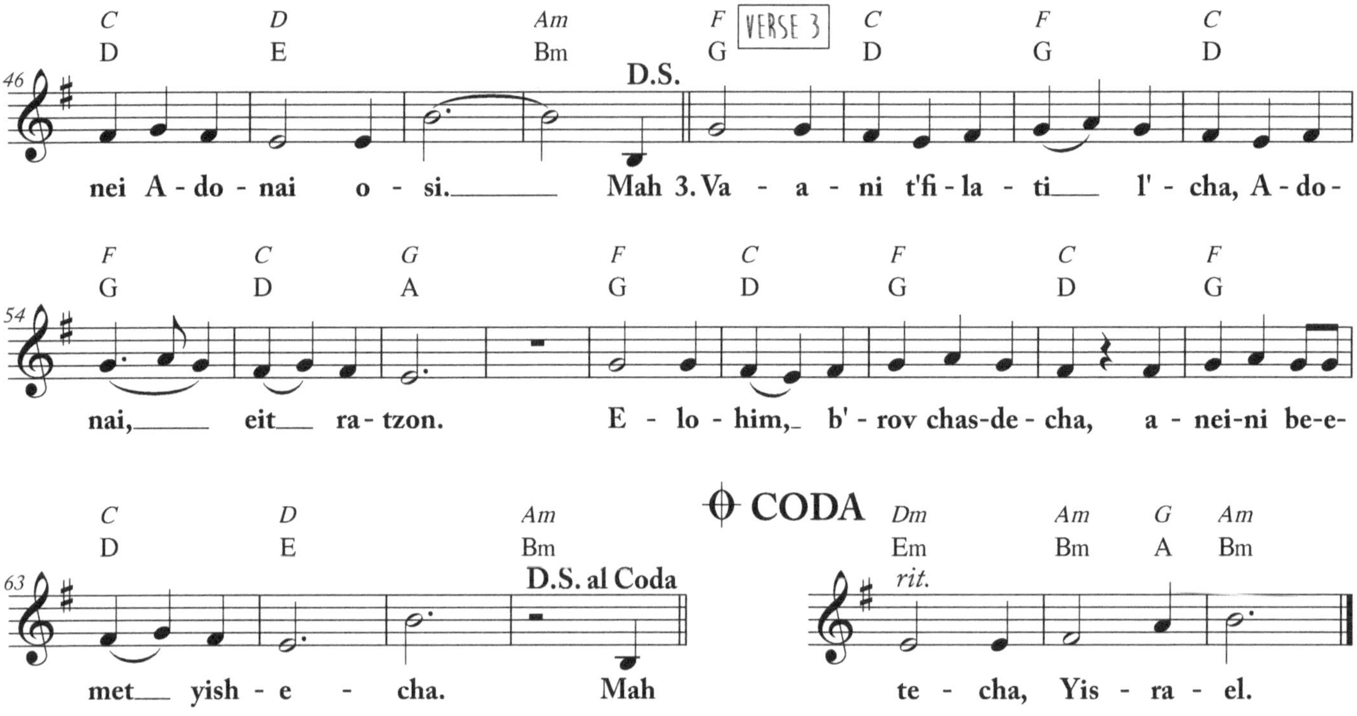

How fair are your tents, O Jacob, your dwellings, O Israel.	מַה־טֹּבוּ אֹהָלֶיךָ, יַעֲקֹב, מִשְׁכְּנֹתֶיךָ, יִשְׂרָאֵל!
I, through Your abundant love, enter Your house; I bow down in awe at Your holy temple.	וַאֲנִי בְּרֹב חַסְדְּךָ אָבוֹא בֵיתֶךָ, אֶשְׁתַּחֲוֶה אֶל־הֵיכַל קָדְשְׁךָ בְּיִרְאָתֶךָ.
Adonai, I love Your temple abode, the dwelling-place of Your glory.	יְיָ, אָהַבְתִּי מְעוֹן בֵּיתֶךָ וּמְקוֹם מִשְׁכַּן כְּבוֹדֶךָ.
I will humbly bow down low before Adonai, my Maker.	וַאֲנִי אֶשְׁתַּחֲוֶה וְאֶכְרָעָה, אֶבְרְכָה לִפְנֵי־יְיָ עֹשִׂי.
As for me, may my prayer come to You, Adonai, at a favorable time. O God, in Your abundant faithfulness, answer me with Your sure deliverance.	וַאֲנִי תְפִלָּתִי לְךָ, יְיָ, עֵת רָצוֹן. אֱלֹהִים, בְּרָב חַסְדֶּךָ, עֲנֵנִי בֶּאֱמֶת יִשְׁעֶךָ.

מי כמכה

MI CHAMOCHAH

MUSIC: AMICHAI SHIRYON
AS SUNG AT KEHILLAT YOZMA (MODI'IN)
TEXT: EVENING LITURGY,
AD. AMICHAI SHIRYON

Who is like You, O God, among the gods that are worshiped?
Who is like You, majestic in holiness,
awesome in splendor, working wonders?

מִי־כָמֹכָה בָּאֵלִם, יְיָ,
מִי כָּמֹכָה נֶאְדָּר בַּקֹּדֶשׁ,
נוֹרָא תְהִלֹּת, עֹשֵׂה פֶלֶא.

Your children witnessed Your sovereignty,
the sea splitting before Miriam (Moses and Miriam).
"This is our God!" they cried.
"Adonai will reign forever and ever!"

מַלְכוּתְךָ רָאָה עַמְּךָ (רָאוּ בָנֶיךָ),
בּוֹקֵעַ יָם לִפְנֵי מִרְיָם (מֹשֶׁה וּמִרְיָם),
זֶה אֵלִי עָנוּ וְאָמְרוּ:
יְיָ יִמְלֹךְ לְעוֹלָם וָעֶד.

Thus it is said, "Adonai redeemed Jacob,
from a hand stronger than his own."
Praised are You, Adonai, for redeeming Israel.

וְנֶאֱמַר: כִּי פָדָה יְיָ אֶת יַעֲקֹב,
וּגְאָלוֹ מִיַּד חָזָק מִמֶּנּוּ.
בָּרוּךְ אַתָּה, יְיָ, גָּאַל יִשְׂרָאֵל.

מי כמכה

MI CHAMOCHAH

Commissioned by Cantor Anna West Ott in honor of Rabbi Bennett Miller of Anshe Emeth Memorial Temple, New Brunswick, New Jersey

MUSIC: OR ZOHAR
ARR. FELIZA BASCARA ZOHAR
FROM HARARIT, MISGAV REGION, THE GALILEE
TEXT: LITURGY, AD. OR ZOHAR

23
Dm Fm
Em Gm
Am Cm
li! a - nu v' - am' - ru: A - do-nai yim - loch l' - o - lam va -
26
C E♭
Em Gm
ed! A - do-nai yim - loch l' - o - lam va - ed! A - do-nai yim -
29
Am Cm
C E♭
Dm Fm
Am Cm
loch l' - o - lam va - ed! A-do-nai yim-loch l' - o - lam va - ed! V'-ne- e -
33
Am Cm
G B♭
Am Cm
mar ki fa - dah A - do-nai et Ya - a - kov, u - g - a -
37
G B♭
Am Cm
lo mi - yad cha-zak mi - me - nu. Ba-ruch a -
41
Am Cm
C E♭
Em Gm
tah, A - do - nai, ga - al Yis - ra - el. Ba-ruch a -
45
Am Cm
C E♭
Dm Fm
Am Cm
continue to Final Chorus, m. 81
tah, A - do - nai, ga - al Yis - ra - el. Mi cha -

MORNING VERSE
49
F Ab C Eb Am Cm Dm Fm
rah cha-da-shah shi-b'-chu g'-u-lim l'-shim-cha al s'fat ha-
52
F Ab Em Gm F Ab C Eb Am Cm
yam. Ya-chad ku-lam ho-du v'-him-
55
Dm Fm Em Gm Am Cm
li-chu v'-am'-ru: A-do-nai yim-loch l'-o-lam va-
58
C Eb Em Gm
ed! A-do-nai yim-loch l'-o-lam va-ed! A-do-nai yim-
61
Am Cm C Eb Dm Fm Am Cm
loch l'-o-lam va-ed! A-do-nai yim-loch l'-o-lam va-ed! Tzur Yis-ra-
65
Am Cm G Bb Am Cm
el, ku-mah b'-ez-rat Yis-ra-el. U-f-
69
G Bb Am Cm
deih chi-nu-me-cha Y'-hu-dah v'-Yis-ra-el. Go-a-

Am Cm C E♭ Em Gm
lei-nu, A-do-nai Tz'va-ot sh'-mo, k'-dosh Yis-ra-el. Ba-ruch a-
Am Cm C E♭ Dm Fm Am Cm
tah, A-do-nai, ga-al Yis-ra-el. Mi cha-
FINAL CHORUS
Am Cm G B♭ Am Cm
mo-chah ba-ei-lim, A-do-nai? Mi ka-
G B♭ Am Cm
mo-chah ne-dar ba-ko-desh, no-ra t'-
Am Cm C E♭ Em Gm
hi-lot, o-seih fe-le, no-ra t'-
Am Cm C E♭ Dm Fm 1. Am Cm 2. Am Cm
last time rit.
hi-lot, o-seih fe-le? no-ra t'-le?

מִי־כָמֹכָה בָּאֵלִם, יְיָ,
מִי כָּמֹכָה נֶאְדָּר בַּקֹּדֶשׁ,
נוֹרָא תְהִלֹּת, עֹשֵׂה פֶלֶא.

Who is like You, O God, among the gods that are worshiped?
Who is like You, majestic in holiness,
awesome in splendor, working wonders?

[Evening]

מַלְכוּתְךָ רָאוּ בָנֶיךָ, רָאוּ בְנוֹתֶיךָ,
בּוֹקֵעַ יָם לִפְנֵי מֹשֶׁה וּמִרְיָם,
זֶה אֵלִי עָנוּ וְאָמְרוּ:
יְיָ יִמְלֹךְ לְעוֹלָם וָעֶד.

Your children witnessed Your sovereignty,
the sea splitting before Moses and Miriam.
"This is our God!" they cried.
"Adonai will reign forever and ever!"

וְנֶאֱמַר: כִּי פָדָה יְיָ אֶת יַעֲקֹב,
וּגְאָלוֹ מִיַּד חָזָק מִמֶּנּוּ.

Thus it is said, "Adonai redeemed Jacob,
from a hand stronger than his own."

[Morning]

שִׁירָה חֲדָשָׁה שִׁבְּחוּ גְאוּלִים
לְשִׁמְךָ עַל שְׂפַת הַיָּם,
יַחַד כֻּלָּם הוֹדוּ וְהִמְלִיכוּ, וְאָמְרוּ:
יְיָ יִמְלֹךְ לְעוֹלָם וָעֶד.

With new song, inspired at the shore of the Sea,
the redeemed sang Your praise.
In unison they all offered thanks. Acknowledging Your sovereignty,
they said: "Adonai will reign forever!"

צוּר יִשְׂרָאֵל, קוּמָה בְּעֶזְרַת יִשְׂרָאֵל.
וּפְדֵה כִנְאֻמֶךָ יְהוּדָה וְיִשְׂרָאֵל.
גֹּאֲלֵנוּ, יְיָ צְבָאוֹת שְׁמוֹ,
קְדוֹשׁ יִשְׂרָאֵל.

Rock of Israel, rise in support of Israel
and redeem Judah and Israel as your promised.
Our Redeemer, *Adonai Tz'vaot*
is Your name.

[Both]

בָּרוּךְ אַתָּה, יְיָ, גָּאַל יִשְׂרָאֵל.

Praised are You, Adonai, for redeeming Israel.

מזמור לדוד

MIZMOR L'DAVID (PSALM 23)

MUSIC: MAYA RAVIV
TEXT: PSALM 23:1, 23:4, AD. MAYA RAVIV

A Psalm of David.
God is my shepherd, I lack nothing.
Even though I walk through the darkest valley,
I will fear no evil for You are with me.

מִזְמוֹר לְדָוִד.
יְיָ רֹעִי, לֹא אֶחְסָר.
גַּם כִּי אֵלֵךְ בְּגֵיא צַלְמָוֶת,
לֹא אִירָא רָע כִּי אַתָּה עִמָּדִי.

שחר אבקשך

SHACHAR AVAKESHCHA

MUSIC: TZVI SHERF
TEXT: SHLOMO IBN GABIROL (11TH C.)

Em7 Am Em7 F G Am
chal ha - leiv v'-ha-la-shon la - a - sot, u - mah ko-ach ru - chi, ru-
Dm E Am Em7 Am Em7
chi v' - toch kir - bi? Hi-neih l'-cha ti - tav zim - rat e - nosh al kein od-
F G7 C D Fmaj7 G 1.Am 2.Am
cha b' - od tih' - yeh nish - mat E - lo - ha bi. bi.
C
Am Em7 Fmaj7(♭5) Em7 Am
Sha-char a - va-kesh-cha tzu - ri u - mis-ga - bi e - e - roch l' - fa-
optional second voice or unison choir
Lu lu lu lu lu lu lu lu lu lu
Em7 Fmaj7(♭5) Em7 Am Em7 Fmaj7(♭5)
ne-cha shach - ri v' - gam ar - bi
lu lu lu lu lu lu lu lu lu lu lu lu lu lu lu lu lu
Em7 F G C D Fmaj7 G Am
ki ein - cha tir - eh, ein - cha tir - eh kol mach - sh'-vot li - bi.
lu lu lu lu lu lu lu lu lu lu

At dawn I seek You, my Rock and Stronghold;
I place before You my morning and evening prayers.
Before Your greatness I stand in awe,
for Your eye sees all my thought.
What can heart
and tongue do,
and what is my spirit's strength within me?
Behold, our human song will gain Your favor.
Therefore I will affirm You
while yet Your spirit lives within me.

שַׁחַר אֲבַקֶּשְׁךָ, צוּרִי וּמִשְׂגַּבִּי
אֶעֱרוֹךְ לְפָנֶיךָ שַׁחְרִי וְגַם עַרְבִּי.
לִפְנֵי גְדֻלָּתְךָ אֶעְמֹד וְאֶבָּהֵל
כִּי עֵינְךָ תִרְאֶה כָּל מַחְשְׁבוֹת לִבִּי.
מַה זֶּה אֲשֶׁר יוּכַל הַלֵּב
וְהַלָּשׁוֹן לַעֲשׂוֹת,
וּמַה כֹּחַ רוּחִי בְּתוֹךְ קִרְבִּי?
הִנֵּה לְךָ תִּיטַב זִמְרַת אֱנוֹשׁ
עַל כֵּן אוֹדְךָ בְּעוֹד תִּהְיֶה
נִשְׁמַת אֱלוֹהַּ בִּי.

שלום על ישראל

SHALOM AL YISRAEL

MUSIC: MAYA RAVIV
TEXT: PSALM 128, AD. MAYA RAVIV

29
D G(add2) Em A(sus4) A
rall.
neih ki chein y' - vo - rach, y' - vo-rach y' - rei A - do - nai.
E
34
D(add2) G(add2) D(add2) G(add2)
a tempo
Ash - rei kol y' - rei A-do-nai ha - ho - leich bid - ra - chav,
38
D(add2) G(add2) D(add2) G(add2)
D.S. al Coda
ash - rei kol y' - rei A-do-nai ha - ho - leich bid - ra - chav.
CODA
42
D G(add2) Em A(sus4) A
neih ki chein y' - vo - rach, y' - vo-rach y' - rei A - do - nai.
F
47
G(add2) A A(sus4) Bm
Y' - va - re - ch'-cha A - do - nai mi - Tzi - yon u - reih b' - tuv Y' - ru - sha - la - yim
50
G(add2) Em7 A(sus4) G(add2) A(sus4) D(sus4) D
kol y'-mei cha-ye - cha. U-reih va-nim l' - va - ne-cha sha - lom al Yis-ra - el.
G
55
Em7 A(sus4) G(add2) A(sus4) D(sus4) D
U - reih va - nim l' - va - ne - cha sha - lom al Yis - ra - el.
60
D(add2) G(add2) D(add2) G(add2) D(add2)
rit.
Ash - rei kol y' - rei A-do-nai ha - ho - leich bid - ra - chav.

SHALOM AL YISRAEL (RAVIV) שלום על ישראל

Blessed are all who are in awe of Adonai	אַשְׁרֵי כָּל־יְרֵא יְיָ
who follow God's ways.	הַהֹלֵךְ בִּדְרָכָיו.
You will eat the fruit of your labor;	יְגִיעַ כַּפֶּיךָ כִּי תֹאכֵל
blessings and prosperity will be yours.	אַשְׁרֶיךָ וְטוֹב לָךְ.
Your spouse will be like a fruitful vine within your house;	אֶשְׁתְּךָ כְּגֶפֶן פֹּרִיָּה בְּיַרְכְּתֵי בֵיתֶךָ
your children will be like olive shoots around your table.	בָּנֶיךָ כִּשְׁתִלֵי זֵיתִים סָבִיב לְשֻׁלְחָנֶךָ.
So shall they who are in awe of God be blessed.	הִנֵּה כִּי־כֵן יְבֹרַךְ יְרֵא יְיָ.
May Adonai bless you from Zion;	יְבָרֶכְךָ יְיָ מִצִּיּוֹן
may you see the prosperity of Jerusalem	וּרְאֵה בְּטוּב יְרוּשָׁלָיִם
all the days of your life,	כֹּל יְמֵי חַיֶּיךָ
and live to see your children's children—	וּרְאֵה־בָנִים לְבָנֶיךָ
Peace be on Israel.	שָׁלוֹם עַל־יִשְׂרָאֵל.

שבורי לב

SHVUREI LEIV

MUSIC AND TEXT: CHANAN BEN ARI AND URIEL WEINBERGER
AS SUNG BY CHANAN BEN ARI

1.Am C F C
Dm F B♭ F
2.Am C Dm Am G Em
Dm F Gm Dm C Am
sof. sof. She-a-ni lo e-ka-na ba-
Am Dm Am Bm7♭5 E7
Dm D Gm Dm Em7(♭5) A7
sof. Na na na na na na na na na na na na na na na na na na na na na na na na
1.Am 2.Am C E F Em
Dm Dm F B♭ Am
na na na na na. Mi, el mi a-ni mit - ga-gei-a
Dm Am C F Em
Gm Dm F B♭ Am
k'mo yam she-ein lo chof? Rak ta-gid li mi, mi y'-cha-beik o-ti v'-yav-ti-ach
Dm Am G Em Am C Dm Am G Em Am
Gm Dm C Am Dm F Gm Dm C Am Dm
rit.
she-a-ni lo e-ka-na ba-sof, she-a-ni lo e-ka-na ba-sof.

מִי יוֹדֵעַ כָּל כְּאֵב?
מִי רוֹפֵא לִשְׁבוּרֵי לֵב?
יוֹצֵר אוֹר וָחֹשֶׁךְ,
עוֹשֶׂה שָׁלוֹם וּמִלְחָמָה.

Who knows every pain?
Who heals all broken hearts?
Creator of light and darkness,
Maker of peace and of war.

מִי יוֹשֵׁב עַל כִּסֵּא דִין
מִתְכַּסֶּה בְּרַחֲמִים?
מוֹחֵל וְסוֹלֵחַ,
מַבִּיט וְיוֹדֵעַ.

Who sits on a throne of judgment
clothed in mercy?
Pardoning and forgiving,
watching and knowing.

וּמִי יְרַפֵּא לִבִּי?
אֶל מִי אֲנִי מִתְגַּעְגֵּעַ
כְּמוֹ יָם שֶׁאֵין לוֹ חוֹף?

And who will heal my heart?
Who do I long for
like a sea without a shore?

רַק תַּגִּיד לִי מִי
מִי יְחַבֵּק אוֹתִי וְיַבְטִיחַ
שֶׁאֲנִי לֹא אֶכָּנַע בַּסּוֹף?

Just tell me who—
who will embrace me and promise
that I will not give up in the end?

מִי הָיָה הֹוֶה וְיִהְיֶה?
מִי מֵמִית וּמְחַיֶּה?
פּוֹתֵחַ יָדַיִם,
מַצְמִיחַ כְּנָפַיִם.

Who was, is, and will be?
Who takes and gives life?
Opening hands,
spreading wings.

תפילת הדרך (הנח לרגלי ללכת)

T'FILAT HADERECH

(HANACH L'RAGLAI LALECHET)

MUSIC: RINA EPSTEIN
TEXT: TAMAR DUVDEVANI

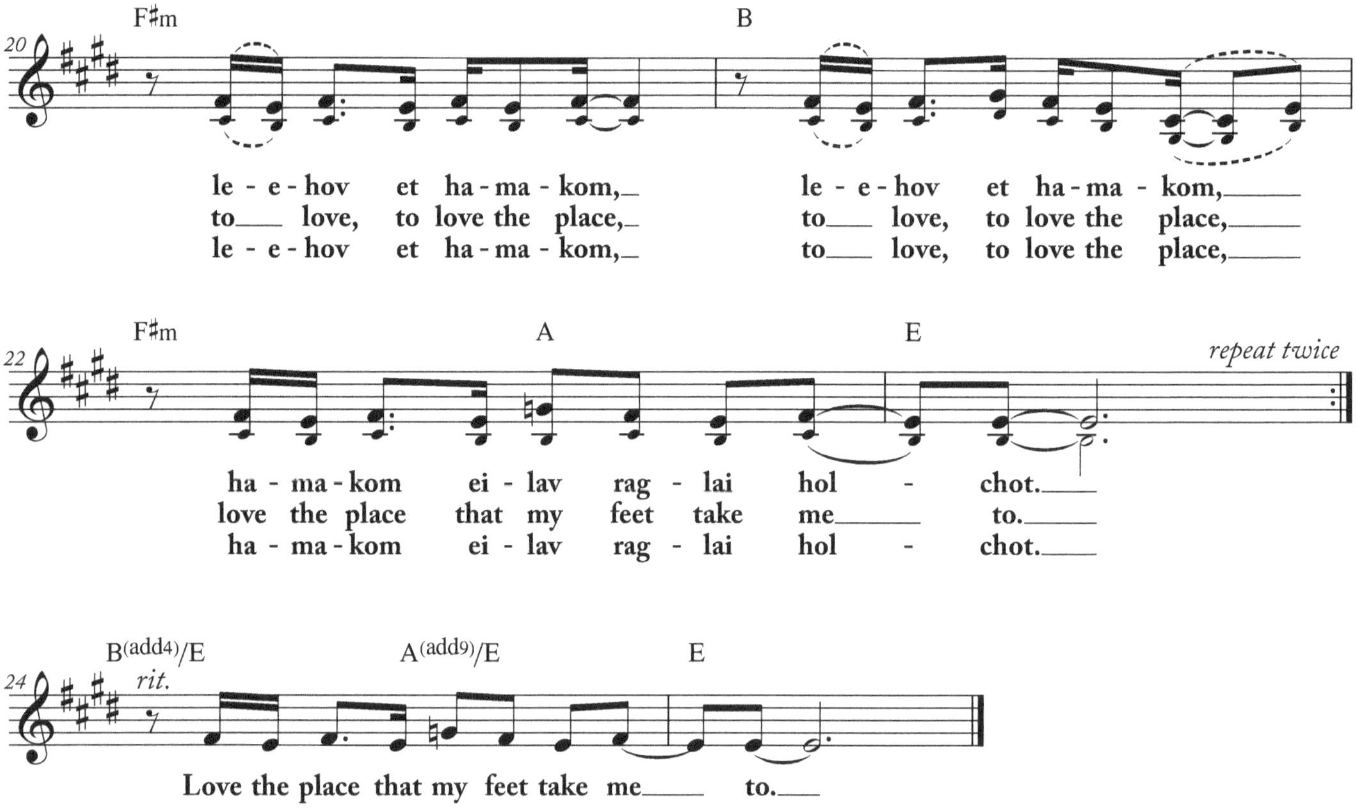

Let me walk
to the place
that my heart loves.
And open my heart to love
the place
that my feet take me to.

הַנַּח לְרַגְלַי לָלֶכֶת
לַמָּקוֹם
שֶׁלִּבִּי אוֹהֵב.
וּפְתַח לִבִּי לֶאֱהֹב
אֶת הַמָּקוֹם
אֵלָיו רַגְלַי הוֹלְכוֹת.

תתפללי עלי

TITPAL'LI ALAI

MUSIC AND TEXT: KALEY HALPERIN

Gmaj7 Em A
lot tik-vah. Tit-pa-l'-li a-lai, tit-pa-l'-li a-lai, tit-pa-l'-
D D/F♯ D G G/F♯ Em
li. M'-bat la-sha-ma-yim, yeish ma-kom b'-ya-
D D/F♯ G G/F♯ Em A
da-yim. M'-bat la-sha-ma-yim, ha-leiv mu-chan k'var l'-
D E Gmaj7 Em
veit. Tit-pa-l'-li a-lai.
A(sus4) Bm
Tit-pa-l'-li a-lai.
Em A
Tit-pa-l'-li a-lai.
D/F♯ A
Tit-pa-l'-li a-lai. Tit-pa-l'-
Em D/F♯ G A D
rit.
li a-lai, tit-pa-l'-li a-lai, tit-pa-l'-li.

Days are good; full to the brink,
no time to stop and think.
Pray for me.

יָמִים עֲמוּסִים בְּטוֹב,
אֵין פְּנַאי לַעֲצֹר לַחְשׁוֹב.
תִּתְפַּלְּלִי עָלַי.

Shofar cries, calls to hush,
kids call, ask, and want for much.
Pray for me.

שׁוֹפָר קוֹרֵא, דּוֹרֵשׁ שְׁתִיקָה,
יְלָדִים מְבַקְּשִׁים דָּבָר מָה.
תִּתְפַּלְּלִי עָלַי.

My eyes to the heavens,
it's a little heavy on the arms.

עֵינַי לַשָּׁמַיִם,
קְצָת כָּבֵד בַּיָּדַיִם.

In the center of the house of prayer,
lips whisper words of hope.
Pray for me.

בְּמֶרְכַּז בֵּית הַתְּפִלָּה,
שְׂפָתַיִם מְמַלְמְלוֹת תִּקְוָה.
תִּתְפַּלְּלִי עָלַי.

A look to the heavens,
there is space between the arms.
A look to the heavens,
the heart is ready for home.

מַבָּט לַשָּׁמַיִם,
יֵשׁ מָקוֹם בְּיָדַיִם.
מַבָּט לַשָּׁמַיִם,
הַלֵּב מוּכָן כְּבָר לְבֵית.

Pray for me.

תִּתְפַּלְּלִי עָלַי.

צמאה נפשי

TZAMAH NAFSHI

MUSIC: OHAD HITMAN, AYA KOREM, KOBI OZ, AND MIKA SADE
AS SUNG BY AYA KOREM
TEXT: AVRAHAM IBN EZRA

CODA

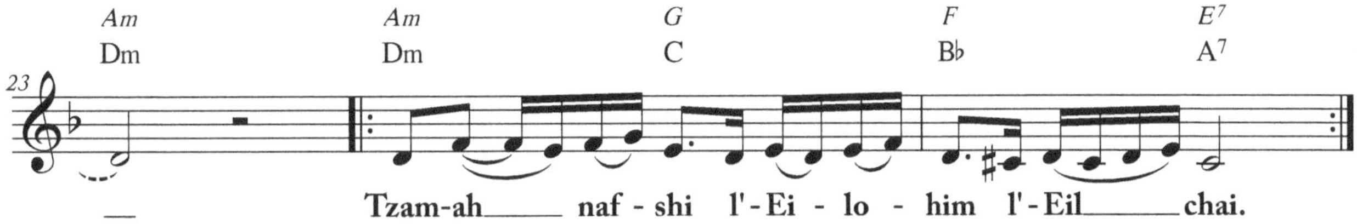

צְמְאָה נַפְשִׁי לֵאלֹהִים לְאֵל חָי,
לִבִּי וּבְשָׂרִי יְרַנְּנוּ לְאֵל חָי.

My soul thirsts for the living God;
my heart and flesh will rejoice for the living God.

אֵל אֶחָד בְּרָאַנִי וְאָמַר חַי אָנִי,
כִּי לֹא יִרְאַנִי הָאָדָם וָחָי.

The One God created me and said, "I live,
for mortals cannot see me and live."

בָּרָא כֹּל בְּחָכְמָה בְּעֵצָה וּבִמְזִמָּה
מְאֹד נֶעְלָמָה מֵעֵינֵי כָּל חָי.
רָם עַל כֹּל כְּבוֹדוֹ
כָּל פֶּה יְחַוֶּה הוֹדוֹ.
בָּרוּךְ אֲשֶׁר בְּיָדוֹ נֶפֶשׁ כָּל חָי.

God created everything with great wisdom, planning, and thought,
hidden from the eyes of all that lives.
God's glory is exalted above everything and
everyone will experience God's majesty.
Blessed is the One in whose hand is the soul of all that lives.

צריך שכל איש ידע ויבין

TZARICH SHEKOL ISH YEIDAH V'YAVIN

MUSIC: MORDECHAI CORCOS
AS SUNG AT KIBBUTZ NEOT SEMADAR
TEXT: ABRAHAM ISAAC KOOK

* *sing small notes second time*

TZARICH SHEKOL ISH YEIDAH V'YAVIN (CORCOS) צריך שכל איש ידע ויבין

צָרִיךְ שֶׁכָּל אִישׁ יֵדַע וְיָבִין
שֶׁבְּתוֹךְ תּוֹכוֹ דּוֹלֵק נֵר,
וְאֵין נֵרוֹ כְּנֵר חֲבֵרוֹ
וְאֵין אִישׁ שֶׁאֵין לוֹ נֵר.
וְצָרִיךְ שֶׁכָּל אִישׁ יֵדַע וְיָבִין
שֶׁעָלָיו לַעֲמֹל וּלְגַלּוֹת
אֶת אוֹר הַנֵּר בָּרַבִּים,
לְהַדְלִיקוֹ לַאֲבוּקָה גְּדוֹלָה
וּלְהָאִיר אֶת הָעוֹלָם כֻּלּוֹ.

Each person must know and understand
that there is a candle lit within them.
And that one person's candle is not like their neighbor's,
and there is no person without a candle.
And each person must know and understand
that it is upon them to labor and to reveal
the light of their candle to the world—
to build it into a great torch
with which to bring light to the whole world.

ואהבת

V'AHAVT

MUSIC: DAPHNA ROSENBERG
FROM NAVA TEHILA (JERUSALEM)
TEXT: BASED ON DEUTERONOMY 6:5, AD. DAPHNA ROSENBERG AND RUTH GAN KAGAN

You shall love Havayah your God
with all your heart, with all your soul,
and with all your might.

וְאָהַבְתְּ אֵת הֲוָיָה אֱלֹהַיִךְ
בְּכָל־לְבָבֵךְ וּבְכָל־נַפְשֵׁךְ
וּבְכָל־מְאֹדֵךְ.

יה רבון עלם

YAH RIBON ALAM

MUSIC: TRADITIONAL IRAQI
TEXT: ISRAEL NAJARA (17TH C.)

1. God of this and all worlds,
You are supreme, the Sovereign God.
Your mighty, wondrous work
moves my heart to praise You.

1. יָהּ רִבּוֹן עָלַם וְעָלְמַיָּא,
אַנְתְּ הוּא מַלְכָּא מֶלֶךְ מַלְכַיָּא.
עוֹבַד גְּבוּרְתֵּךְ, וְתִמְהַיָּא,
שְׁפַר קֳדָמַי, לְהַחֲוָיָא.

2. I will offer praises morning and night,
For You, holy God, who has created all life,
holy beings and humans,
animals on land and birds in the sky.

2. שְׁבָחִין אֲסַדֵּר צַפְרָא וְרַמְשָׁא,
לָךְ אֱלָהָא קַדִּישָׁא דִּי בְרָא כָּל נַפְשָׁא,
עִירִין קַדִּישִׁין וּבְנֵי אֱנָשָׁא,
חֵיוַת בְּרָא וְעוֹפֵי שְׁמַיָּא.

3. Great and mighty are Your deeds,
humbling the proud and raising the humble.
Even if one were to live a thousand years,
they would still not be able to fathom Your might.

3. רַבְרְבִין עוֹבְדֵיךְ וְתַקִּיפִין,
מָכֵין רָמַיָּא וְזָקִיף כְּפִיפִין,
לוּ יְחִי גְבַר שְׁנִין אַלְפִין
לָא יֵעוֹל גְּבוּרְתָךְ בְּחֻשְׁבְּנַיָּא.

4. O God, to whom glory and greatness belong,
save Your flock from the lions' jaws.
Bring Your people out of exile,
the people You chose from among all nations.

4. אֱלָהָא דִּי לֵהּ יְקָר וּרְבוּתָא,
פְּרֵק יַת עָנָךְ מִפֻּם אַרְיָוָתָא,
וְאַפֵּיק יַת עַמָּךְ מִגּוֹ גָלוּתָא,
עַמָּא דִּי בְחַרְתְּ מִכָּל אֻמַּיָּא.

5. Return to Your Temple and to the Holy of Holies,
the place where spirits and souls can rejoice.
They will sing to You songs and melodies
in Jerusalem, city of beauty.

5. לְמִקְדָּשֵׁךְ תּוּב וּלְקֹדֶשׁ קֻדְשִׁין,
אֲתַר דִּי בֵהּ יֶחֱדוּן רוּחִין וְנַפְשִׁין,
וִיזַמְּרוּן לָךְ שִׁירִין וְרַחֲשִׁין,
בִּירוּשְׁלֵם קַרְתָּא דְשׁוּפְרַיָּא.

יעלה יעלה

YA'LAH YA'LAH

MUSIC: TRADITIONAL MOROCCAN
AS SUNG AT KEHILLAT YOZMA (MODI'IN) ED. BE'AYIN MIZRACHIT
TEXT: ISRAEL NAJARA (16TH C.)

O my doe, O my doe, come to my garden;
the pomegranates are in bloom and my vines have flowered.

יַעְלָה, יַעְלָה, בּוֹאִי לְגַנִּי,
הֵנֵץ רִמּוֹן גַּם פָּרְחָה גַּפְנִי.

1. Come, my Beloved, hasten Your steps;
eat of the sweet fruits.
If my Lover's wanderings have been drawn out,
how shall I sit alone in my place?

1. יָבוֹא, דוֹדִי, יָחִישׁ צְעָדָיו
וְיֹאכַל אֶת פְּרִי מְגָדָיו.
אִם יְדִידִי אָרְכוּ נְדוּדָיו
אֵיךְ יְחִידָה אֵשֵׁב עַל כַּנִּי.

2. Return to Me, most beloved;
return to Me and I shall return to you.
Behold I have with Me written proof
that you shall be My dwelling place.

2. שׁוּבִי אֵלַי, אַתְּ בַּת אֲהוּבָה,
שׁוּבִי אַתְּ וַאֲנִי אָשׁוּבָה.
הִנֵּה עִמִּי זֹאת אוֹת כְּתוּבָה
כִּי בְּתוֹכֵךְ אֶתֵּן מִשְׁכָּנִי.

3. My Friend, my Beloved, You have redeemed my soul
and have since taken me to be Your wife.
And now among other nations You have dispersed me,
so how can You say that You love me?

3. רֵעִי, דּוֹדִי, נַפְשִׁי פָּדִיתָ
וּלְבַת מֵאָז אוֹתִי קָנִיתָ.
עַתָּה לִי בֵּין עַמִּים זֵרִיתָ
וְאֵיךְ תֹּאמַר כִּי אֲהַבְתָּנִי.

4. My awesome one, it is for the best that I dispersed you;
your struggle is for your glory and benefit.
For My love for you is eternal,
thus I will seat you upon My dais.

4. אֲיֻמָּתִי, לְטוֹב זֵרִיתִיךְ
וְלִתְהִלָּה וּלְטוֹב שָׂרִיתִיךְ.
כִּי אַהֲבַת עוֹלָם אֲהַבְתִּיךְ
עַל כֵּן אוֹשִׁיבֵךְ עַל דּוּכָנִי.

5. May it be as You say, my Love,
now quickly bring my wanderings to an end.
And into Zion lead my troops
and there I will offer my sacrifice to You.

5. לוּ יְהִי כִדְבָרְךָ, יְדִידִי,
עַתָּה מַהֵר תֶּאֱסֹף נְדוּדִי.
וּלְתוֹךְ צִיּוֹן נְחֵה גְדוּדִי
וְשָׁם אַקְרִיב לְךָ אֶת קָרְבָּנִי.

6. Be strengthened, My wife, your mouth is like the choicest wine;
for the bud of My saving power is fresh and juicy.
Your enemies I will fell and cut down
and I will speedily send you My messenger.

6. חִזְקִי, רַעְיָה, חִכֵּךְ כְּיֵין טוֹב
כִּי צִיץ יִשְׁעִי רַעֲנָן וְרָטוֹב.
וּלְסִירַיִךְ אֶכְרוֹת וְאֶחְטֹב
וְחִישׁ אֶשְׁלַח לָךְ אֶת סְגָנִי.

ידיד נפש

Y'DID NEFESH

MUSIC: TRADITIONAL MOROCCAN
AS SUNG AT KEHILLAT YOZMA (MODI'IN) ED. BE'AYIN MIZRACHIT
TEXT: ELEZAR BEN MOSES AZIKRI (16TH C.)

B
Am Dm
av - dach k' - mo a - yal, ya-rutz av - dach k' - mo a - yal yish - ta - cha -
Eil na r' - fa na lah, a - na Eil na r' - fa na lah, b' - har - ot
cha - meh nich - sof nich - saf, ki zeh cha - meh nich - sof nich - saf, lir - ot b' -
e - retz mi - k - vo - dach, ta - ir e - retz mi - k - vo - dach, na - gi - lah
C F Dm Gm
veh el mul ha - da - rach. Ki ye - e - rav lo y' - di - du - tach, mi - no - fet
lah___ no - am zi - vach. Az tit - cha - zeik v' - tit - ra - pei, v' - hay'-tah
tif - e - ret u - zach. A - na, Ei - li, mach - mad li - bi, chu-shah na
v' - nis - m' - chah vach. Ma-heir, a - huv, ki va mo - eid, v' - cho - nei -
G C Dm Gm
tzuf v'-chol ta - am, ki ye - e - rav lo y' - di - du - tach, mi - no - fet
lah sim-chat o - lam, az tit - cha - zeik v' - tit - ra - pei, v' - hay'-tah
v' - al tit - a - lam, a - na Ei - li, mach - mad li - bi, chu-shah na
ni ki - mei o - lam, ma-heir, a - huv, ki va mo - eid, v' - cho - nei -
F B♭ Em Am Am Dm
tzuf___ v'-chol___ ta - am,___ ki ye - e - rav lo y' - di - du - tach, mi - no - fet
lah___ sim-chat___ o - lam,___ az tit - cha - zeik v' - tit - ra - pei, v' - hay'-tah
v' - al tit - a - lam,___ a - na Ei - li, mach - mad li - bi, chu-shah na
ni___ ki - mei___ o - lam,___ ma-heir, a - huv, ki va mo - eid, v' - cho - nei -
G C Dm Gm
tzuf v' - chol ta - am, ye - e - rav lo y' - di - du - tach, mi - no - fet
lah sim - chat o - lam, az tit - cha - zeik v' - tit - ra - pei, v' - hay'-tah
v' - al tit - a - lam, a - na Ei - li, mach - mad li - bi, chu-shah na
ni ki - mei o - lam, ma-heir, a - huv, ki va mo - eid, v' - cho - nei -

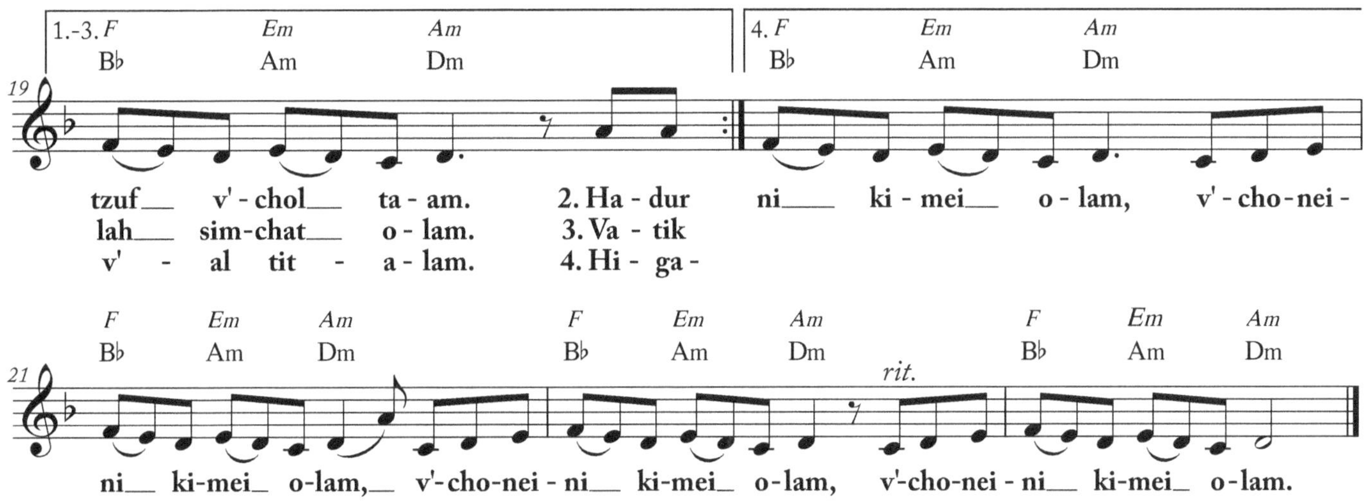

1. Heart's delight, Source of mercy,
draw Your servant into Your arms.
I leap like a deer
to stand in awe before You.
Your love is sweeter to me
than the taste of honey.

1. יְדִיד נֶפֶשׁ, אָב הָרַחֲמָן,
מְשׁוֹךְ עַבְדְּךָ אֶל רְצוֹנָךְ.
יָרוּץ עַבְדְּךָ כְּמוֹ אַיָּל
יִשְׁתַּחֲוֶה מוּל הֲדָרָךְ.
כִּי יֶעֱרַב לוֹ יְדִידוּתָךְ,
מִנֹּפֶת צוּף וְכָל טָעַם.

2. World's light, shining glory,
my heart is faint for love of You.
Heal it, O God; help my heart;
show me Your radiant splendor.
Let me return to strength
and have joy for ever.

2. הָדוּר נָאֶה, זִיו הָעוֹלָם,
נַפְשִׁי חוֹלַת אַהֲבָתָךְ.
אָנָּא אֵל נָא, רְפָא נָא לָהּ,
בְּהַרְאוֹת לָהּ נֹעַם זִיוָךְ.
אָז תִּתְחַזֵּק וְתִתְרַפֵּא,
וְהָיְתָה לָהּ שִׂמְחַת עוֹלָם.

3. Have compassion, O Faithful One,
pity for Your loved child.
How long have I hoped
to see Your glorious might.
O God, my heart's desire,
have pity and hold back no more.

3. וָתִיק, יֶהֱמוּ רַחֲמֶיךָ,
וְחוּסָה נָא עַל בֵּן אוֹהֲבָךְ.
כִּי זֶה כַּמֶּה נִכְסֹף נִכְסַף
לִרְאוֹת בְּתִפְאֶרֶת עֻזָּךְ.
אָנָּא, אֵלִי, מַחְמַד לִבִּי,
חוּשָׁה נָּא וְאַל תִּתְעַלָּם.

4. Show Yourself, Beloved, and cover me
with the shelter of Your peace.
Light up the world with Your Presence
that we may exult and rejoice in You.
Hurry, Loved One, the appointed time has come.
Show us grace as long ago.

4. הִגָּלֶה נָא, וּפְרֹשׂ, חָבִיב עָלַי,
אֶת סֻכַּת שְׁלוֹמָךְ.
תָּאִיר אֶרֶץ מִכְּבוֹדָךְ;
נָגִילָה וְנִשְׂמְחָה בָּךְ.
מַהֵר, אָהוּב, כִּי בָא מוֹעֵד,
וְחָנֵּנִי כִּימֵי עוֹלָם.

יהיו לרצון

YIH'YU L'RATZON

MUSIC: OR ZOHAR
ARR. FELIZA BASCARA ZOHAR
FROM HARARIT, MISGAV REGION, THE GALILEE
TEXT: LITURGY

Gently, with rhythm ♩ = 92

Optional second voice or choir

יִהְיוּ לְרָצוֹן אִמְרֵי־פִי
וְהֶגְיוֹן לִבִּי לְפָנֶיךָ,
יְיָ, צוּרִי וְגוֹאֲלִי.

עֹשֶׂה שָׁלוֹם בִּמְרוֹמָיו,
הוּא יַעֲשֶׂה שָׁלוֹם עָלֵינוּ,
וְעַל כָּל יִשְׂרָאֵל, וְעַל כָּל תֵּבֵל.
וְאִמְרוּ: אָמֵן.

May the words of my mouth
and the meditations of my heart be acceptable to You,
Adonai, my Rock and my Redeemer.

May the one who makes peace in the high heavens
make peace for us,
all Israel, and all who inhabit the earth.
Amen.

יונתי

YONATI

MUSIC: NAVOT BEN BARAK
TEXT: SONG OF SONGS 2:14

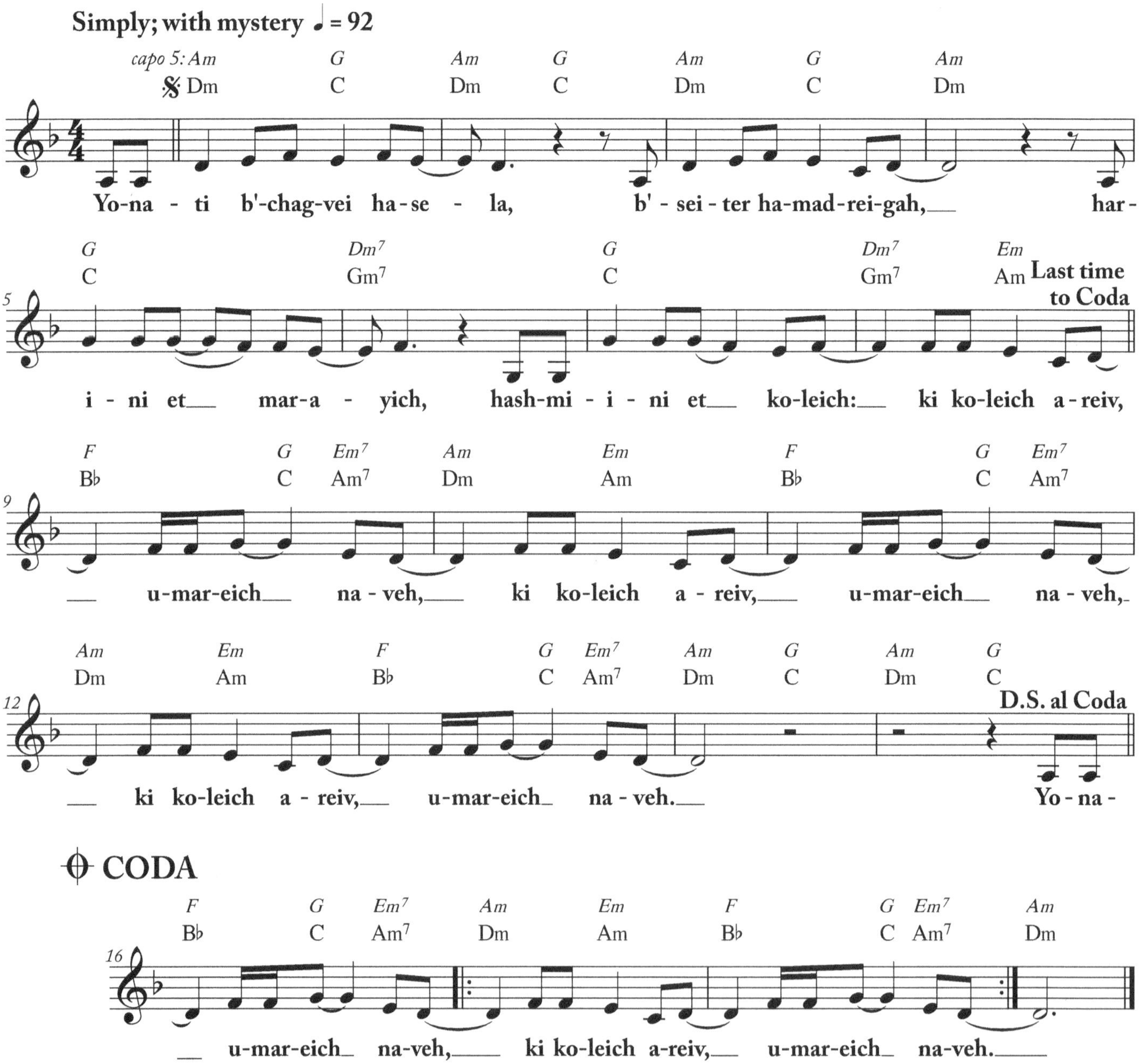

O my dove, in the crevice of the rock,
concealed by the mountain's face,
show me your countenance,
let me hear your voice:
for your voice is pleasant,
and your countenance charming.

יוֹנָתִי בְּחַגְוֵי הַסֶּלַע,
בְּסֵתֶר הַמַּדְרֵגָה,
הַרְאִינִי אֶת־מַרְאַיִךְ,
הַשְׁמִיעִינִי אֶת־קוֹלֵךְ:
כִּי־קוֹלֵךְ עָרֵב,
וּמַרְאֵיךְ נָאוֶה.

יושב בסתר עליון

YOSHEIV B'SEITER ELYON

MUSIC: SAVION BEN ISRAEL
TEXT: PSALM 91:1, 2, 4, 5, 10, 12, 9,
AD. SAVION BEN ISRAEL

Am F E
e-ven rag-le-cha. Lo t'-u-neh ei-le-cha ra-ah v'-
E7 Am Dm
ne-ga lo yik-rav b'-o-ho-le-cha. Al ka-pa-yim yi-sa-un-cha
E7 Am Am/G D F G
pen ti-gof ba-e-ven rag-le-cha. Ki a-tah A-do-nai mach-si El-
C C♯o Dm E E+ E7 Am Am(add9) 5fr
yon sam-ta m'o-ne-cha. Lo ti-ra mi-pa-chad
E Dm Am
lai-lah mei-cheitz ya-uf yo-mam. Lo ti-ra mi-
F Dm6 E rall.
pa-chad lai-lah mei-cheitz ya-uf yo-mam. Al ka-
Dm E7 Am
pa-yim yi-sa-un-cha pen ti-gof ba-e-ven rag-le-cha.
E F E E7
Lo t'-u-neh ei-le-cha ra-ah v'-ne-ga lo yik-rav b'-o-ho-

You who dwell in the shelter of the Most High
and abide in the protection of Shaddai:

יֹשֵׁב בְּסֵתֶר עֶלְיוֹן
בְּצֵל שַׁדַּי יִתְלוֹנָן.

I say of Adonai, my refuge and stronghold,
my God in whom I trust,

אֹמַר לַייָ מַחְסִי וּמְצוּדָתִי
אֱלֹהַי אֶבְטַח־בּוֹ.

God will cover you with God's pinions;
you will find refuge under God's wings.

בְּאֶבְרָתוֹ יָסֶךְ לָךְ
וְתַחַת כְּנָפָיו תֶּחְסֶה.

You need not fear the terror by night,
or the arrow that flies by day.

לֹא־תִירָא מִפַּחַד לָיְלָה
מֵחֵץ יָעוּף יוֹמָם.

They [God's angels] will carry you in their hands
lest you hurt your foot on a stone.

עַל־כַּפַּיִם יִשָּׂאוּנְךָ
פֶּן־תִּגֹּף בָּאֶבֶן רַגְלֶךָ.

No harm will befall you,
no disease touch your tent,

לֹא־תְאֻנֶּה אֵלֶיךָ רָעָה
וְנֶגַע לֹא־יִקְרַב בְּאָהֳלֶךָ.

because you took Adonai—my refuge,
the Most High—as your haven.

כִּי־אַתָּה יְיָ מַחְסִי
עֶלְיוֹן שַׂמְתָּ מְעוֹנֶךָ.

THE SONGWRITERS AND COMMUNITIES

Photograph by Ephrat Beloosesky

JONATHAN (YONATAN) BAR GIORA is an Israeli pianist, composer, and musical producer-arranger. Since 2000, Bar Giora has composed for over 150 Israeli films including *Bonjour Monsieur Shlomi*, *Time of Favor*, *Queen Shoshana*, *Salech Po Ze Eretz Israel*, *Aviva, My Love,* and many others. He also worked as a composer with Israeli performers such as Yossi Banai, Rita, Miri Mesika, Ester Rada, Meir Banai, Alon Eder, and many others. During 2011-15 Bar Giora was the head of the department of film music and sound design in the School of Audio & Visual Arts at Sapir Academic College, where he is now the head of the BFA program. He also lectures at Beit Berl's film school and at the Maaleh School of Film and Television.

NAVOT BEN BARAK is a musician, a spiritual care provider (CPE), and a yoga teacher. He is a composer of traditional Jewish liturgical music and a leader of musical ceremonies around the Jewish life cycle. In his work as a healing musician and spiritual care provider (chaplain), his compositions focus on healing and revitalizing melodies for various verses from Psalms, *Shir HaShirim* (Song of Songs), *t'filah* (prayers), and more. He has released the albums *Journey in the Song of Songs*, *Shirey Refua* (through the Haverut organization), and *Stars in Heaven*.

RABBI GOLAN BEN-CHORIN Ed.D., a third-generation Israeli Reform rabbi, entrepreneurial educator, and spiritual leader, believes Judaism is a language for leading a life of meaning. Having founded two Reform communities in Israel and worked in Jewish leadership across five continents, he developed Netivei Midrash—multiple intelligence gateways to Judaism. In response to COVID-19, he began producing documentaries as a means of sharing his Jewish teaching, while his movie *Dinking Across Faith: A Cross-Cultural Pickleball Documentary* earned him the title of first rabbi to appear in *Sports Illustrated*. Utilizing his doctoral work on pluralism, he is a practitioner of both formal and informal Jewish education and a deep believer in the power of music to stir the soul and awaken the spirit. He now serves as senior rabbi at Alyth in London, one of the largest Reform congregations in Europe.

המלחינים והקהילות

SAVION BEN ISRAEL is an independent researcher of consciousness and spirituality and a musician. She has composed music for film, children's plays, meditative movement, poetry, and the Jewish holidays. Although she is secular, Savion has a special fondness for composing *piyutim* (religious poetry in song), texts from prayers, and music for Song of Songs text. She lived in a kibbutz for many years, ran the local school, and taught children music and composition. Currently living in Tel Aviv, she studies mind-body therapies and drawing and conducts an orchestra at the Rimon School of Music.

Cantor-Rabbi **SHANI BEN-OR** is the first person to become a Reform ordained cantor in Israel. Her home congregation is Kehilat Kol HaNeshama in Jerusalem. She has served in cantorial roles in Israel and around the world, as the cantorial soloist of the United Jewish Congregation in Hong Kong and as student cantor of Central Synagogue in New York. Shani received her dual ordination as a cantor and rabbi from Hebrew Union College–Jewish Institute of Religion in Jerusalem and New York. Shani is an active member of the Israel Movement for Reform and Progressive Judaism (IMPJ), both as a professional and lay leader. In 2013, she established T'lamim, a community of young Reform Jewish adults in Israel. Together with Boaz Dorot, she is the co-founder of the Nigunim Ensemble, a pioneering ensemble that creates, arranges, and performs sacred music to accompany religious services throughout Israel. Today Shani runs the Ashkenazi track of Ashira Tehilot at the Schechter Institute Rabbinical School, a hub for community leaders focused on prayer and music. She is also head of multicultural programing at Hebrew University, with an emphasis on initiatives bridging gaps between east and west Jerusalem. Shani aspires to establish a thriving liberal cantorate in Israel—one that is authentic and relevant to the multicultural climate of Israeli society, is fluent in the musical treasures of Ashkenaz and Mizrachi Jewish traditions, and creates music for a variety of sacred spaces and occasions that are unique to Eretz Yisrael.

MORDECHAI CORCOS, born in Israel in 1960, is a metal and silversmith artist at the Kibbutz Neot Semadar art center. Mordechai is also a musician and a composer of contemporary and ancient texts from Jewish literature throughout the ages. At the community of Neot Semadar, Mordechai leads meditative, musical, and movement events. Mordechai is one of the founders of the kibbutz, which is located in the southern Aravah desert. The community he helped establish seeks a life with personal and social significance. Central to their ethos is the practice of introspection both individually and collectively, forming the cornerstone of community life. Mordechai currently holds the role of community manager at Neot Semadar.

THE SONGWRITERS AND COMMUNITIES

BOAZ DOROT is a composer, arranger, choir conductor, and pianist. His original compositions and arrangements have been performed all around Israel and the West. Boaz is the recipient of the 2018 Guild of Temple Musicians Young Composer's Award. He was raised in Kehilat Kol HaNeshama in Jerusalem and has been involved with the Israel Movement for Reform and Progressive Judaism (IMPJ) since early childhood. Today, he serves as the musical director of Kehilat Kol HaNeshama and is also involved nationally with IMPJ, directing music, composing for *t'filah* (prayers), conducting choirs, and supervising music in prayer services. Boaz is the co-founder of the Nigunim Ensemble, a pioneering ensemble that creates, arranges, and performs sacred music to accompany religious services throughout Israel.

RINA EPSTEIN, born 1987 in Jerusalem, grew up in the Kol HaNeshama congregation as well as the Telem (Reform) youth movement in Israel. Music, spirituality, and caring for the earth have always been her passions. She completed the Telem gap year leadership program before joining the IDF, and after her military service she worked in South Africa as a delegate (*sh'lichah*) through the Jewish Agency for the Reform youth movement in Cape Town (Netzer). Rina has been a songleader, composer, and songwriter in many different settings including sacred singing circles, High Holy Day alternative song sessions for young adults in the Reform Movement in Israel, and independent musical projects. In the past decade, her main focus has been on environmentalism, sustainability, and permaculture. She has traveled the world working, volunteering, and visiting many communities and farming projects. Today, she manages an organic small-scale farm in Israel and teaches sustainable agricultural and permaculture courses.

KALEY HALPERIN is an American-born singer-songwriter and community activist from Jaffa, Israel. With a voice reminiscent of folk singers from the 1960s and '70s, Kaley's music is a mix of American folk, traditional Jewish music, and sounds from around the world. She strives with her music and workshops to bring people closer to themselves, to one another, and to their higher power. With a bachelor's degree in music education and master's degree in Jewish studies and various programs in music and prayer, Kaley uses her learned skills of crowd inclusion and group learning to create spaces of togetherness and inquiry for all ages. Kaley has released music that is played on Israeli radio and Jewish stations around the world. She has performed all around Israel in festivals and venues ranging from large theaters to intimate living room concerts. Her song "Titpal'li Alai" (Pray for Me) has become part of prayer and singing circles in communities in Israel and the United States. Her community activism includes a renewal and leading of a welcoming community in an old synagogue in Jaffa, heading projects in Jewish culture and communities for the Tel Aviv municipality, and being the artistic director for Jaffa Choses Life, a collective of Jewish and Arabic artists that puts the spotlight on community and culture in Tel Aviv mixed neighborhoods.

VERED IVTSAN was born in Haifa, Israel. She is a certified nurse and cantorial soloist and active as a guitarist and songwriter. Music flows through her veins: her father, a Holocaust survivor, was a cantor and music teacher. He instilled in Vered a deep love for Jewish music and prayers from a young age. Music has been Vered's companion through life's joys and sorrows; in happy moments and difficult times, melodies and lyrics pour out of her. She finds inspiration from the people she cherishes and from her prayers. As a nurse, Vered connects the body and soul. She teaches the Feldenkrais method of mindful movement. With a holistic approach, she nurtures the whole person through music and healing practices. Vered was a central part of the Or Hadash synagogue community in Haifa, leading services there for years, and participated in a cantorial-training course to further her Jewish musical education. She has shared her musical gifts while raising her four daughters and is now a proud grandmother of four. Vered's voice and spirit continue to uplift her community.

AYA KOREM, singer, songwriter, and composer, was born in 1980 in Nazareth Illit, Israel. After serving in the army as a tank instructor, she attended college at the Rimon School of Contemporary Music. Korem's debut, self-titled album was released in 2006 and received gold record status. The album was followed by seven additional studio albums, including numerous hits, while Korem had been continuously performing throughout Israel and abroad. In July 2009, she joined the ensemble My Favorite Enemy, an unlikely collaboration between well-known musicians from Israel, Jordan, the West Bank, and Europe. The group recorded an album and went on tour in the Middle East, Europe, and the United States, including shows at the UN and at the National Prayer Breakfast in Washington, DC. Having fought a long battle for independence from her record label, in 2014 Korem initiated a law proposal to eliminate draconian contracts from the Israeli music industry. This proposal was accepted by the Israeli parliament and in February 2017 became a law that bears Aya's name. Today she resides with her family in Jaffa and writes a weekly column in Israel's most popular daily publication, *Israel Hayom*. She continues to create music with her partner, producer, and guitarist Adam Ben Amitai.

THE SONGWRITERS AND COMMUNITIES

Photograph by Shalom Shayovitz

THE NAVA TEHILA COMMUNITY (JERUSALEM)

Nava Tehila is a Jerusalem-based Jewish renewal spiritual community. They specialize in creating musical and engaging prayer spaces where people feel comfortable to come as they are. Nava Tehila's musical spiritual leaders generate new prayer modalities, compose new music for prayer, and train Jewish leaders, including rabbis, cantors, and students, in the art of musical and innovative prayer leading. They have composed over 120 melodies for prayer and produced three albums of original music: *Dancing in the Glory*, *Waking Heart*, and *HAVAYAH*. Visit www.NavaTehila.org for more information.

Photograph by Ilan Bashor

MAUREEN NEHEDAR is a vocal artist, composer, and *paytanit* (singer of Jewish liturgical poems), a poetess and researcher of Jewish musical traditions in general and particularly of the Judeo-Persian tradition. She is a pioneer of the world-music scene in Israel and a pioneer in the renewal of Jewish music known throughout the world. She has revived the Judeo-Persian poetical and liturgical tradition, saving them from oblivion. Maureen has won many awards, the most prominent of which is the 2023 Uri Orbach Prize for Jewish Culture in the Field of Music in Israel. Maureen has released four highly successful albums, which have received excellent critical reviews, thus positioning her as one of the most important singers and artists in Israeli music. Maureen is at the "top of the premier league of female singers in Israel," as music critic Ben Shalev wrote in *Haaretz*.

Israeli composer, performer, and educator **MAYA RAVIV** breathes new life into ancient Hebrew texts, combining universal themes from the Jewish tradition with the healing power of music to connect to the larger human experience. Born and raised in Israel and educated in the United States, Maya has absorbed the sounds and stories of many faiths, all of which have influenced her life's work. Maya has carried out her mission performing for Iraqi refugees in Jordan, for Holocaust survivors in Oklahoma, at Lincoln Center and the United Nations headquarters, and in churches and synagogues across America. In 2007, she returned to Israel's western Galilee region and dedicated her musical work to the families of those lost to war, performing at the Israeli Defense Forces national memorial services, and for the campaign for the release of hostage Gilad Schalit, until his release in 2011. From 2009 to 2013 Maya was the composer-in-residence for the Society for Universal Sacred Music and served as a member of its board of directors. Maya holds a master's degree in music composition and a bachelor's degree in vocal performance from Oklahoma City University. Since 2012, Maya's work has been dedicated to her Psalms Project, composing prayers from the ancient Hebrew psalms and leading workshops of emotional healing. Her albums include *To the Eagle*, *Echad*, and *Tfilati*. In 2022, Maya was honored to sing her compositions from the psalms at Israel's National Memorial Day ceremony in the National Memorial Hall, on Mount Herzl in Jerusalem. mayaraviv.com

המלחינים והקהילות

DAPHNA ROSENBERG is a singer, guitarist, and composer. She was the co-founder and the main prayer leader of Nava Tehila for eighteen years and traveled extensively to share, present, and teach the Nava Tehila *t'filah b'tzibur* musical methods around the Jewish world. She composes original music to prayers and poetry and specializes in musically leading life-cycle ceremonies. Daphna serves in the area of spiritual care for the ill and dying, supporting bereaved families and creating heart-to-heart connections between people from different cultures and traditions. She is currently a student in water-based emotional therapy, under the auspices of Tel Hai College.

TZVI SHERF, born in 1948, is an Israeli composer, songwriter, arranger, and choral conductor. Among his many recorded songs is the popular and highly appreciated "Haduda'im," first performed in the Israeli Hasidic Song Festival of 1979. He is best known for his choral arrangements, most of them of popular Hebrew, Ladino, and folk songs, as well as traditional *piyutim* and *nigunim*. Tzvi's arrangements have been commissioned by some of the most well-known Israeli choirs, including the Israeli Vocal Ensemble, the Bertini Choir, Moran, Efroni, Bat Kol, Na'ama, and more, and by Israeli choral organizations Zimriya and Hallel. Many of them have been recorded by his ensemble, Coral Ensemble. His music is available at www.tzvi-sherf.com, popular with many choirs in Israel and all over the world.

RUTI SOKOLOFF grew up in Herzliya and Sde Boker, Israel, and discovered her love for both the piano and the desert at a very a young age. She studied classical piano at the Rubin Academy and musicology at Hebrew University, and earned an MA in music therapy at the David Yellin Academy in Jerusalem. She plays klezmer and Chasidic music, performs with improvisational playback theater groups all over Israel, and practices as a music therapist. Ruti has five children and thirteen grandchildren and lives in Efrat and Yerucham.

THE SONGWRITERS AND COMMUNITIES

TANDU (loosely translated from Aramaic as "togetherness") is a unique band of musicians who combine songs and *piyutim* (Jewish liturgical folk music) from East and West, traditional texts alongside contemporary arrangements, original compositions, and "mashups" in Hebrew and English. The ensemble is led by Shani and Yahala Lachmish—sisters, musicians, singers, and composers. Music flows through their veins; their professional path began as children singing on stage with their mother and grandmother (as the Simcha Girls) in performances all over Israel. Shani and Yahala founded Tandu in 2013 with the aim of touching hearts. The music they create is harmonious, sometimes rhythmic, and sometimes all-embracing. A performance of Tandu, with their uplifting music and charismatic presentation, brings out smiles, raises spirits, and warms and comforts the hearts and souls of their audiences, whether live or virtual. Tandu's vibe incorporates world music, "falafel jazz," soul, and of course *piyut*.

YONI AND NINA TOKAYER, also known as **YONINA**, are an Israeli-American musical duo acclaimed for their weekly home videos, which have reached millions of viewers around the globe. They have released two original albums and perform throughout Israel and Jewish communities abroad. Yoni and Nina have been singing together since they met and married in 2015, and they now have four sweet children, who make guest appearances in their videos. Known for their positive music and soft harmonies, Yonina create a blend between Jewish, Israeli, and international music.

THE KEHILLAT YOZMA COMMUNITY (MODI'IN)

The YOZMA community in Modi'in, Israel, seeks to offer a Jewish progressive and pluralistic alternative, to encourage the public to take initiative and define its Jewish identity, and to help the Israeli public form a meaningful and valuable connection to Judaism in these times and to see the beauty, holiness, and spirituality that modern Judaism can offer. This is all done by redefining what we know as "Israeli music," and turning it into an experience that touches the spiritual heart and soul.

The **BE'AYIN MIZRACHIT** ensemble was born out of a desire to expand the tent sheets of the eastern *piyut* in the Reform houses of prayer and to make room for everyone, to pave the way for one to walk in prayer, and to enable a significant means of expressing the Jewish identity of each and every person. Their music honors prayer traditions passed down from generation to generation. The members of the group, who come from Reform backgrounds (most of them from the YOZMA congregation in the city of Modi'in), bring with them the spirit of the young leadership of the next generation in the Reform Movement. The members of the Be'ayin Mizrachit are Shani Milo (keyboard and vocals), Alon Marom (percussion), Noya Kislanski (bass, guitar, vocals), Gal Adir Stern (guitar, baglama, vocals), Yuval Iluz (oud), and Rabbi David Azoulay (vocals). They perform throughout Israel.

AMICHAI SHIRYON, is the son of Rabbi Kinneret Shiryon and Baruch Shiryon, *z"l*, founders of Kehillat YOZMA. Amichai grew up a child of YOZMA's community. He picked up the guitar at a young age (with his father being his first guitar teacher) and soon found himself to be an aspiring musician. Amichai holds a BA in music from the Jerusalem Academy of Music and Dance. He also was a *shaliach* (emissary) and a *madrich* and songleader for the Jewish Agency in the United States (OSRUI). Amichai is working as an independent musician in Israel, teaching music and instruments to both young and adult students, and performing around the country in jazz, rock, folk, and traditional Irish ensembles. For many years, he has been accompanying and composing for YOZMA's *Kabbalat Shabbat* services. He is a member of YOZMA's music ensemble.

BARUCH SHIRYON, *z"l*, (1954–2016), was an Israeli composer. As a young man he taught himself music and how to play the guitar. Baruch was a self-taught, accomplished *ketubah* artist for many years, a warm family man, and he had a love for photography. Baruch was a founding member of Kehillat YOZMA in Modi'in, Israel. He accompanied the *Kabbalat Shabbat* service with his guitar for over twenty years in collaboration with his wife, Rabbi Kinneret Shiryon. His creative talents in integrating modern Israeli melodies and his original musical compositions into the services enriched the YOZMA community's prayer experience. After his untimely death, the sanctuary of YOZMA was dedicated in his memory and named Ma'ayan Baruch (a Blessed Spring). His music, talent, humility, kindness, commitment, and warm personality were a spring of blessing for all who came in his path.

THE SONGWRITERS AND COMMUNITIES

FELIZA AND OR ZOHAR are a sacred music duo from the Galilee region. They tour internationally, sharing their music, teachings, and life experiences, and collaborate with local clergy, musicians, and choirs. Feliza and Or have released three albums of sacred music: *Lev Tahor*, *Mikolot Mayim*, and *Kets Haplaot*. Their fourth album, consisting of new original compositions of sacred Jewish music, is forthcoming. The Zohars' sacred music tells a contemporary story of Israel, the Jewish people, and the human spirit. Or Zohar is a Reform rabbi, singer-songwriter, Kabbalah scholar, and founder of the Spirit of the Galilee Association. Ordained by Hebrew Union College–Jewish Institute of Religion in Jerusalem, he has served as a Reform rabbi of the Misgav Region in the Galilee. He is now senior rabbi of Temple Sinai in Rochester, New York. Feliza Bascara-Zohar is a multidisciplinary artist, a mover, a choreographer, a performance artist, and a singer-songwriter. Her art aspires to see the divine in everyday life and to experience prayer as a spiritual-embodied practice. She has a bachelor's degree in musicology and literature from the Hebrew University of Jerusalem and a master's degree in expressive arts from Tel Aviv University.
www.orandfelizamusic.com

LIBI B'MIZRACH SERIES INDEX

VOLUME	TITLE	COMPOSER
II	Adonai Malach	Micha Biton
III	Adon HaS'lichot	Traditional Sephardic (Y'rushalmi)
III	Adon Olam	Baruch Shiryon
III	Adon Olam	From Algerian Song "Ya Rayeh"
III	Ahuvi	Yonatan Bar Giora
III	Al Ahavatecha Eshteh G'vi-i	Shani Ben-Or and Boaz Dorot
III	Am Echad	Ariel Zurayev, Yehuda Kaplan, and Yonatan Girtz
I	Ana B'choach	Navot Ben Barak
II	Ashrei Ha-ish	Maya Raviv
III	B'chol Dor Vador	Mordechai Corcos
II	Dirshu Adonai	Yonatan Niv
II	D'ror Yikra	Margalit Jakob
III	Eil Adon	Ruti Sokoloff
I	Eil Na R'fa Na Lah	Or Zohar
II	Eili Atah V'odeka	Atalya Lavi
I	Hal'luyah	Yoel Sykes
I	Hal'luyah Mima'amakim	Or Zohar
III	Hal'luyah (Psalm 150)	Daphna Rosenberg
III	Haneirot	Vered Ivtsan and Avital Ben-Chorin
III	Haor MiTziyon	Kaley Halperin
II	Hashkiveinu	Savion Ben Israel
I	Hegyon Libi	Shimon Smith
I	Ilu Finu	Shlomo Gronich
I	Into the West Nigun	Yoel Sykes
I	Ivdu	Or Zohar
II	Kanfei Ruach	Avigail Uziel Amar
II	Ki Beiti Beit T'filah	Shlomo Gronich
III	Ki Eshm'rah Shabbat / V'sham'ru	Traditional Moroccan
III	Ki Simachtani	Daphna Rosenberg and Ruth Gan Kagan
III	Kiryah Y'feihfiyah	Maureen Nehedar
III	Kol Chamira	Kaley Halperin
II	Kumi Ori	Shimon Smith
III	Lamdeini	Maya Raviv
III	Lamdeini	Yonatan Tokayer
I	Lamdeini / Bar'chu	Yonatan Niv
II	Lam'natzei-ach	Gilad Hazan
II	L'cha Adonai / Rom'mu	Daphna Rosenberg
I	L'chah Dodi	Navot Ben Barak
II	L'chah Dodi	Micha Biton
II	L'chah Dodi	Margalit Jakob
III	L'chah Dodi	Maureen Nehedar
I	L'chah Dodi	Daphna Rosenberg
III	L'chah Dodi	Traditional Sephardic (Y'rushalmi)
II	L'chah Dodi	Or Zohar

מפתח סדרות

VOLUME	TITLE	COMPOSER
II	L'chu N'ran'nah	Or Zohar
III	L'eil Oreich Din	Daphna Rosenberg and Ruth Gan Kagan
II	Leiv Tahor	Maya Raviv
III	Lo Yisa Goi	Daphna Rosenberg and Yoel Sykes
III	Mah Navu Alei	Traditional Iraqi
III	Mah Tovu	Baruch Shiryon
III	Mi Chamochah	Amichai Shiryon
III	Mi Chamochah	Or Zohar
II	Min Hameitzar Karati	Michal Talya
III	Mizmor L'David	Maya Raviv
I	Mizmor Shir	Kayla Dinis
I	Mizmor Shir	Daphna Rosenberg
I	Nigun Chagigi	Yotam Mahler
II	Nishmat Kol Chai	Yoel Sykes
II	Pitchu Li	Feliza Bascara-Zohar
I	Pure Heart	Daphna Rosenberg and Yoel Sykes
I	R'fa Tziri	Traditional Sephardic
II	Salachti Kidvarecha	Porat Nov
I	S'fatai Tiftach / Oseh Shalom	Beit Tefilah Israeli
II	Sha-alu Sh'lom Y'rushalayim	Eyal Bat
III	Shachar Avakeshcha	Tzvi Sherf
II	Shalom Aleichem	Navot Ben Barak
II	Shalom Aleichem	Margalit Jakob
II	Shalom Aleichem	Baruch Shiryon
III	Shalom Al Yisrael	Maya Raviv
II	Shir Hamaalot	Margalit Jakob
III	Shvurei Leiv	Chanan Ben Ari and Uriel Weinberger
I	Sim Shalom	Daphna Rosenberg
III	T'filat Haderech (Hanach L'raglai Lalechet)	Rina Epstein and Tamar Duvdevani
III	Titpal'li Alai	Kaley Halperin
III	Tzamah Nafshi	Ohad Hitman, Aya Korem, Kobi Oz, and Mika Sade
II	Tzam'ah Nafshi	Michal Talya
III	Tzarich Shekol Ish Yeidah V'yavin	Mordechai Corcos
III	V'ahavt	Daphna Rosenberg
II	Yadati	Margalit Jakob
II	Yah Anah Emtza-acha	Meirav Meshulem Levy
III	Yah Ribon Alam	Traditional Iraqi
III	Ya'lah Ya'lah	Traditional Moroccan
III	Y'did Nefesh	Traditional Moroccan
III	Yih'yu L'ratzon	Or Zohar
III	Yonati	Navot Ben Barak
I	Yonati	Shani Ben-Or and Boaz Dorot
III	Yosheiv B'seiter Elyon	Savion Ben Israel
II	Yotzeir Or	Shani Ben-Or and Boaz Dorot
II	Zamru	Micha Biton

TRACK LIST FOR ACCOMPANYING ALBUM

רשימת השירים לאלבום הנלווה

1. **Adon HaS'lichot (Traditional Sephardic)** **
   Performed by Be'ayin Mizrachit
2. **Adon Olam (B. Shiryon)**
   Performed by Amichai Shiryon
3. **Adon Olam (From "Ya Rayeh")** **
   Performed by Be'ayin Mizrachit
4. **Ahuvi (Bar Giora)** *
   Performed by Cantor Galit Dadoun Cohen
5. **Al Ahavatecha Eshteh G'vi-i (Ben-Or/Dorot)**
   Performed by Nigunim Ensemble
6. **Am Echad (Zurayev/Kaplan/Girtz)** *
   Performed by Cantor Iris Karlin
7. **B'chol Dor Vador (Corcos)**
   Performed by Mordechai Corcos
8. **Eil Adon (Sokoloff)**
   Performed by Ruti Sokoloff
9. **Hal'luyah (Psalm 150) (Rosenberg)** ***
   Performed by Daphna Rosenberg
10. **Haneirot (Ivtsan/Ben-Chorin)**
    Performed by Vered Ivtsan and Golan Ben-Chorin
11. **Haor MiTziyon (Halperin)**
    Performed by Kaley Halperin
12. **V'sham'ru (Traditional Moroccan)** **
    Performed by Be'ayin Mizrachit
13. **Ki Simachtani (Rosenberg/Gan Kagan)** ***
    Performed by Daphna Rosenberg
14. **Kiryah Y'feihfiyah (Nehedar)**
    Performed by Maureen Nehedar
15. **Kol Chamira (Halperin)**
    Performed by Kaley Halperin
16. **Lamdeini (Raviv)**
    Performed by Maya Raviv
17. **Lamdeini (Tokayer)**
    Performed by Yonina
18. **L'chah Dodi (Nehedar)**
    Performed by Maureen Nehedar
19. **L'chah Dodi (Traditional Sephardic)** **
    Performed by Be'ayin Mizrachit
20. **L'eil Oreich Din (Rosenberg/Gan Kagan)** ***
    Performed by Daphna Rosenberg
21. **Lo Yisa Goi (Rosenberg/Sykes)**
    Performed by Nava Tehila
22. **Mah Navu Alei (Traditional Iraqi)**
    Performed by Tandu
23. **Mah Tovu (B. Shiryon)**
    Performed by Amichai Shiryon
24. **Mi Chamochah (A. Shiryon)**
    Performed by Amichai Shiryon
25. **Mi Chamochah (Zohar)**
    Performed by Or and Feliza Zohar
26. **Mizmor L'David (Raviv)**
    Performed by Maya Raviv
27. **Shachar Avakeshcha (Sherf)**
    Performed by Tzvi Sherf
28. **Shalom Al Yisrael (Raviv)**
    Performed by Maya Raviv
29. **Shvurei Leiv (Ben Ari/Weinberger)** *
    Performed by Cantor Iris Karlin
30. **T'filat Haderech (Hanach L'raglai Lalechet) (Epstein/Duvdevani)**
    Performed by Rina Epstein, Shani Ben-Or, and Noa Tal-El
31. **Titpal'li Alai (Halperin)**
    Performed by Kaley Halperin
32. **Tzamah Nafshi (Hitman/Korem/Oz/Sade)** *
    Performed by Cantor Iris Karlin
33. **Tzarich Shekol Ish Yeidah V'yavin (Corcos)**
    Performed by Mordechai Corcos
34. **V'ahavt (Rosenberg)** ***
    Performed by Daphna Rosenberg
35. **Yah Ribon Alam (Traditional Iraqi)**
    Performed by Global Piyut Project
    Used by permission of B'nai Jeshurun (New York, New York)
36. **Ya'lah Ya'lah (Traditional Moroccan)** **
    Performed by Be'ayin Mizrachit
37. **Y'did Nefesh (Traditional Moroccan)** **
    Performed by Be'ayin Mizrachit
38. **Yih'yu L'ratzon (Zohar)**
    Performed by Or and Feliza Zohar
39. **Yonati (Ben Barak)**
    Performed by Navot Ben Barak
40. **Yosheiv B'seiter Elyon (Ben Israel)**
    Performed by Savion Ben Israel

Recordings executive produced by TMP exclusively for this volume:
* Produced by Joel Eglash; engineered by Collin Stanley (Mirrortone Studio remote recording). Recorded May 2024 at Congregation Beit Simchat Torah (New York, New York). Mixed and mastered by Joel Eglash and Collin Stanley. Piano: Scott Stein (6, 29, 32) and Joyce Rosenzweig (4).
** Produced by Be'ayin Mizrachit; executive produced by Joel Eglash. Recorded May 2024 at Rafsoda Tachtit Studio (Tel Aviv, Israel). Mixed by Yuval Iluz. Piano/vocals: Shani Milo, percussion/vocals: Alon Marom, bass/vocals: Noya Kislanski, guitar/vocals: Gal Adir Stern, oud/vocals: Yuval Iluz, vocals: Rabbi David Azoulay.
*** Produced by Daphna Rosenberg; executive produced by Joel Eglash. Engineered and mixed by Shlomi Mor. Recorded April 2024 at Shlomi Mor Recording Studio (Pardes Hana, Israel). Guitar/vocals: Daphna Rosenberg, guitar/percussion: Shlomi Mor.